Ibrahim El-Salahi

Prison Notebook

Edited by
Salah M. Hassan

The Museum of Modern Art, New York

Sharjah Art Foundation

Ibrahim El-Salahi (Sudanese, born 1930)
Prison Notebook. 1976
Notebook with thirty-nine ink-on-paper drawings,
page: 11 5/16 x 6 11/16 in. (28.7 x 17 cm)
The Museum of Modern Art, New York. Acquired through the generosity of Marlene Hess and James D. Zirin, Catie and Donald Marron, Alice and Tom Tisch (in honor of Christophe Cherix), Marnie Pillsbury, and Committee on Drawings and Prints Fund, 2017

Produced by the Department of Publications,
The Museum of Modern Art, New York
Christopher Hudson, Publisher
Don McMahon, Editorial Director
Marc Sapir, Production Director

Editor: Salah M. Hassan

AT THE MUSEUM OF MODERN ART
Edited by Maria Marchenkova and Rebecca Roberts
Designed by Amanda Washburn
Production by Matthew Pimm
Coordinated by Sarah Suzuki

AT SHARJAH ART FOUNDATION
Managing Editor: Ahmad Makia
Publication Coordinators: Shannon Ayers-Holden and Wasan Yousif
Translators (Arabic to English): Mustafa Adam and Adil Ibrahim Babikir
Editorial Consultant: Karen Marta
Project Consultant: Todd Bradway

Printed and bound by Verona Libri, Verona, Italy

This book is typeset in Eldorado and Figgins.
The paper is 90 gsm Fly Gelblichweiss.

Published by The Museum of Modern Art,
11 West 53 Street, New York, New York, 10019-5497,
www.moma.org, and Sharjah Art Foundation,
Al Shuwaiheen, Arts Area, Sharjah, United Arab Emirates, PO Box 19989, www.sharjahart.org

© 2018 The Museum of Modern Art, New York, and Sharjah Art Foundation. Works by Ibrahim El-Salahi are © 2018 Ibrahim El-Salahi/Artists Rights Society (ARS), New York/DACS, London.
All rights reserved.

Distributed in the United States and Canada by
Artbook | D.A.P.
75 Broad Street, Suite 630
New York, New York 10004
www.artbook.com

Distributed in the United Arab Emirates by
Sharjah Art Foundation
Al Shuwaiheen, Arts Area, Sharjah
United Arab Emirates, PO Box 19989
www.sharjahart.org

Distributed in the rest of the world by
Thames & Hudson Ltd
181A High Holborn, London WC1V 7QX
www.thamesandhudson.com

Library of Congress Control Number: 2018942357

ISBN: 978-1-63345-055-4

Printed in Italy

Contents

The Prison Notebook *begins on the last page of this volume and is read from right to left, as is conventional for Arabic writings. Turn the book over to begin.*

Foreword

THE SUDANESE ARTIST IBRAHIM EL-SALAHI WAS arrested in September 1975 and held without trial for six months in Khartoum's notorious Kober Prison, wrongfully accused of involvement in an anti-government coup. In the weeks of house arrest that followed his release, the pioneering modernist artist, intellectual, and teacher produced his *Prison Notebook*. Modest in scale but immeasurable in impact, this sketchbook of masterful pen-and-ink drawings and virtuoso prose and poetry in Arabic served both to exorcise and document his experience behind bars. Now, more than four decades later, the volume finds itself at the forefront of cultural conversations, assuming its rightful place as a masterwork of African and Arabic modernism. It was included in the 2012–13 exhibition *Ibrahim El-Salahi: A Visionary Modernist*, organized by the Museum for African Art, New York (now the Africa Center), in association with the Tate Modern, London, which premiered at the Sharjah Art Museum in May 2012 and traveled to the Katara Cultural Village Foundation, in Doha, Qatar, in October 2012. More recently, the *Prison Notebook* was central to the groundbreaking exhibition *The Khartoum School: The Making of the Modern Art Movement in Sudan (1945–Present)*, mounted at the Sharjah Art Foundation in 2016–17. The Sharjah Art Foundation and The Museum of Modern Art are proud to be partners in this facsimile edition of El-Salahi's *Prison Notebook*, which brings the artist's unforgettable images and writings to a broad, English-speaking audience for the first time.

We are deeply grateful to Ibrahim and Katherine El-Salahi for their interest in this project and their devotion to its production. Salah M. Hassan, the editor of this volume, deserves our thanks for conceiving this extraordinary publication and for sharing his profound knowledge of El-Salahi's work with our readers in his essay in these pages. Sarah Suzuki, Curator of Drawings and Prints at The Museum of Modern Art, and Judith Greer, Director of International Programmes at the Sharjah Art Foundation, were critical in shepherding the volume to completion.

The publishing teams at both institutions have been models of cooperation, working together to produce this technically complex reproduction of the *Prison Notebook* as well as the texts that illuminate it for English readers. At The Museum of Modern Art, Christopher Hudson, Publisher, spearheaded the collaboration between our two institutions; Marc Sapir, Production Director, and Matthew Pimm, Production Manager, ensured that the remarkable nuance of El-Salahi's work was brilliantly reproduced; Amanda Washburn, Senior Designer, conceived the book's elegant design; and Rebecca Roberts, Editor, and Maria Marchenkova, Assistant Editor, played key roles in the preparation of the texts.

At the Sharjah Art Foundation, Ahmad Makia, Managing Editor, oversaw the collaboration between our two institutions; Wasan Yousif, Publication Coordinator, and Shannon Ayers-Holden, former Publication Coordinator, performed essential transcription of the artist's commentary and ensured that the Arabic writings in the *Prison Notebook* were translated into the most representative English. For the translation, they worked with Mustafa Adam and Adil Ibrahim Babikir, who produced a splendid version of El-Salahi's writings, capturing their beauty and specificity. We are grateful to Karen Marta, editorial consultant, for guiding us through the publishing of this special volume. Finally, we would like to express our gratitude to Toby Clarke, director of Vigo Gallery, London, which represents the artist, for his efforts in making the reproduction of the *Prison Notebook* a possibility. It is our great pleasure to share this extraordinary work with our audiences, and we look forward to future collaborations between our institutions.

Glenn D. Lowry, Director
The Museum of Modern Art

Hoor Al Qasimi, President and Director
Sharjah Art Foundation

Ibrahim El-Salahi's *Prison Notebook*
A Visual Memoir

Salah M. Hassan

THE LAST THREE DECADES HAVE WITNESSED the publication of numerous prison memoirs by former political prisoners in Sudan, and a number of testimonials about torture and human rights abuses have been produced in pamphlets or as open letters addressed to the authorities and the public. These publications complement reports issued by local and international human rights organizations but differ markedly from them in their emphasis on the personal legacy of political incarceration in Sudan.[1] The authors, who tend to be intellectuals and activists and are mostly leftist in their political leanings, have borne the brunt of political oppression in Sudan from colonial days and through the various national regimes, including both dictatorial and democratically elected governments.

The intellectual and political contribution of these memoirs and testimonials is immense, precisely due to their expansion of the public debate around both the demons of the past and the prevalent human rights abuses of the present, which include the torture, incarceration, and illegal detention of pro-democracy activists. Most imperatively, they call for the constitution of a national truth-and-reconciliation commission to address this horrific legacy, a prerequisite to a truly democratic Sudan. Yet what is most intriguing about these writings is the picture they paint of the prison experience as lived, witnessed, and narrated by the incarcerated subject-authors. They open our eyes to the prison as a space of resistance, political education, consciousness raising, and intellectual nourishment, which, ironically, stands in stark contrast to its conception as an institutional site for punishment, repentance, or reform.[2]

All of these Sudanese prison memoirs are works of writing alone, with one conspicuous exception: the *Prison Notebook* of Ibrahim El-Salahi, the pioneer modernist painter and visionary Sudanese intellectual who endured an extended period of incarceration in the mid-1970s during the regime of military dictator Gaafar Nimeiri (1969–85).[3] El-Salahi created a series of delicate, visually intriguing pen-and-ink drawings in a sketchbook during his house arrest in 1976, after his release from Khartoum's infamous Kober (Cooper) Prison.[4] Both aesthetically and in the context of their making, they recall the prison drawings of the early-twentieth-century Austrian painter Egon Schiele, despite the different factors that led to their respective incarcerations.[5] Both artists expressed their anguish and personal trauma by recording their prison experiences: Schiele in watercolor drawings in which emaciated human figures contrast with stark prison walls, and El-Salahi in delicate and meticulous black-and-white pen-and-ink drawings that combine a visual documentation of the day-to-day prison experience with hauntingly surreal self-portraits, brief stream-of-consciousness poetry, prose, and prayers, and short Qur'anic verses.

THE CARCERAL REGIME IN POSTCOLONIAL SUDAN

There is no doubt that the carceral regime in postcolonial Sudan is very much embedded in the British colonial penal regime that preceded it, if it is not an outright continuation of it. In 1956, soon after Sudan achieved independence, the colonial penal regime was subjected to a series of reforms based on the modernist European ideal of prisons as spaces of rehabilitation rather than retribution and punishment.[6] Among other changes, this involved the introduction of educational opportunities for prisoners (mostly vocational, as a way of preparing them for post-prison life); access to health care and mental health counseling and to radio, books, and newspapers; and, for less violent criminals who weren't considered flight risks, supervised release time in which to work and earn a living, provided they returned at night to sleep in prison. The origins and fate of these reforms have been the subject of contestation within the scarce but growing body of scholarship on incarceration in postcolonial Sudan. Abdullahi Ali Ibrahim has written that these attempts at evolving away from the colonial carceral system soon failed, a result of their "artificiality" and their shallow roots in the country.[7] In contrast, W. J. Berridge has argued that the post-independence reforms were at least temporarily successful: "The reform-minded carceral system that existed from the 1950s to 1960s was not a mere legacy of colonial rule; rather, the modernizing Sudanese prison professionals of this era developed the prison system far beyond the infrastructure that had existed previously and espoused educationalist and civilizational ideals with an alacrity unseen in the colonial era."[8] This Berridge has termed "defensive developmentalism": in their efforts, the modernizing nationalists tried not only to "demonstrate their capacity to govern their own country" but also to adapt reformist prison ideals to their own cultural norms.[9] Both scholars agree, however, that there was an eventual shift from reform and rehabilitation to retribution and punishment in the prisons of postcolonial Sudan. This merits further investigation, but it is embedded in the rise of the military regime and of one-party systems in Sudan, which mirrored similar shifts taking place in postcolonial Africa and the Arab world beginning in the mid-1970s.

General Nimeiri's military regime ruled Sudan from 1969 to 1985, when the famous popular uprising ushered in democratic rule. This lasted until 1989, when a short-lived multiparty parliamentary experiment was usurped through a military coup that brought to power the current Islamist regime, one of the most repressive and murderous in Sudanese history. Prison reforms were slowly abandoned beginning in the mid-1970s, as Nimeiri prioritized political survival over serious development programs that would value human rights and basic civil liberties. In its evolution into a one-party, Nasserist-style system of governance, the regime opted for consolidation of power. It subjected the population to austerity programs imposed by the International Monetary Fund and the World Bank, which eventually led to the decline of the national economy, the further privatization of the public sector, and the rise of corruption and the looting of state and national resources. These developments were further complicated by the continuation of the North-South civil war, which would eventually lead to the partition of Sudan and the creation of the Republic of South Sudan in 2011.[10] In this context, Berridge has argued, "the government became less concerned with governing its subjects than with demonstrating its physical power over them."[11] She elaborates:

The shift towards more corporeal, deterrent and retributive forms of punishment occurred in the context of racial and religious ideologies which stigmatized the inhabitants of Sudan's peripheries and denied them the capacity for moral and social reformation. Just as the state moved from rehabilitative policies towards physical deterrence in dealing with conventional criminals, the use of extreme forms of violence against political prisoners became more acceptable. In both cases, this shift towards a more violent and deterrent form of asserting the regime's authority underlined the frailties of the prison system and the state's inability to exert pervasive forms of social and political control.[12]

As the repressive state security organ grew and its authority expanded, an ultra-judicial system arose, and prisons were expanded to hold political prisoners.[13] The housing of political and conventional prisoners together tends to facilitate the spreading of democratic and anti-military ideas and to increase communication between political prisoners and the world beyond the prison walls. Political prisoners in the Sudan at that time were mainly activists, intellectuals, and trade unionists—people generally skilled at organizing in any milieu, even in prison. In addition, as modernist prison-reform regulations dictated at the time, conventional prisoners were afforded legal rights that the ruling regime and its security organs did not wish to extend to political prisoners. This eventually led to the creation of two separate categories within the prison population, and spatial segregation was maintained (at least in principle) between the two types.

PRISON RESISTANCE CULTURE IN POSTCOLONIAL SUDAN

El-Salahi has never been a member of a leftist political party or, for that matter, of any other political party in Sudan. That said, like many intellectuals of his generation, he could not avoid leftist ideas, which have had a commanding presence in Sudan since the 1940s, or their impact on the political public sphere.[14] Most relevant to this essay is the interesting role the Sudanese Left has played in transforming the country's prison culture. As we learn from published prison memoirs, the security system within the prison ward in this period was in practice quite porous; the separation of the two populations was not absolute. Conventional prisoners engaged in mutually beneficial and symbiotic relationships with political prisoners and were able to move between what appeared to be separate, well-guarded spaces. For example, conventional detainees were known to smuggle messages, medicine, and food to political prisoners. It is also well-known that prison guards tended to sympathize with political prisoners, for reasons ranging from political and ethnic affiliations to familial relationships to simple human empathy with their causes. Prison professionals such as officers and soldiers engaged in similar relationships with political prisoners and, unlike security officers, avoided torturing or mistreating them, knowing that the political terrain might change: the prisoner of today might be in power tomorrow.

Conventional prisoners had more rights, although the treatment of political prisoners by Nimeiri's regime fluctuated in severity, sometimes harsher (restriction of access to the media, the press, books, and contact with the outside world), sometimes gentler. Imprisoned Sudanese leftists and Marxist activists engaged in collective bargaining on behalf of political prisoners, and they consistently put pressure on prison authorities and security organs to improve their conditions and their access to the outside world. They organized themselves into committees around daily needs and demands, and they introduced the concept of the "commune," a system whereby supplies such as soap, cigarettes, toothpaste, clothing, and other basic necessities were collected in order to be redistributed equally among all political prisoners. They were also known for discreetly building small libraries; books were smuggled in via sympathetic prison guards and officers and through networks of families and sympathizers. In addition, they instituted daily sports and physical exercise routines to help break the monotony of confinement and keep up their morale and health. For example, the late Abdel Karim Mirghani, former ambassador to India, offered yoga classes to prisoners in the 1970s. They also organized classes in all fields of knowledge as well as programs of singing, theater, and other forms of entertainment, exploiting the talent and expertise of the political prisoners themselves, most of whom were highly educated. Many Sudanese political leaders wrote seminal texts during incarceration. The most formidable example is Abdel Khaliq Mahgoub, secretary of the Sudanese Communist Party, who produced several of his major books during periods of solitary confinement in Kober Prison in the late 1950s and early 1960s.[15]

Because of this effective construction of community, many former political prisoners have said that they found it emotionally difficult to leave prison and, in fact, had tears in their eyes as they left. Such mixed emotions are testimony to the camaraderie that political prisoners developed in transforming the prison into a place of knowledge, community, and solidarity in the struggle for democracy. Sudanese political prisoners also helped organize contact with the outside world. They kept their causes alive and publicized their demands by engaging in hunger strikes and other acts of resistance, usually accomplished through their highly organized underground movement. This came to be known in the literature of the underground Sudanese Left as "creating cracks in the walls of the dictatorship"—prisoners used social relations and traditions as potent forms of critique, targeting the intolerable cruelties that were inflicted on them with impunity and an utter lack of remorse.[16] It is crucial to point out that elements of the leftist tradition in Sudanese prisons have been borrowed by other political groups in the country and even emulated by imprisoned members of right-wing parties.

EL-SALAHI'S POST-PRISON WORK

El-Salahi is one of the most impressive figures in contemporary African art. He is an artist whose productivity has spanned more than five decades, and he is a powerful intellectual who remains morally conscientious, socially concerned, and uncompromising in his artistic integrity. His contributions to the modern African art movement can be measured in many ways: the remarkable quality of his work (primarily painting), his intellectual engagement as an artist and a writer and poet; and his record as a teacher to a generation of Sudanese and other African and Arab diasporic artists. Born in 1930 in the historic city of Omdurman, Sudan, El-Salahi attended the School of Design at Gordon Memorial College (subsequently the Khartoum School of Fine and Applied Art) between 1948 and 1954, where he majored in painting. Between 1954 and 1957 he studied at the Slade School, London. Eventually he returned to Sudan, where he taught for many years at the Khartoum School of Fine and Applied Art, one of the most active centers of creative talent in Africa and a major contributor to the growth of modern art on the continent. It was under the leadership of El-Salahi that the Khartoum School emerged as an important group of artists, known for their distinct, innovative styles. For modern African visual art, El-Salahi is on par with literary giants such as Wole Soyinka, Chinua Achebe, Ngũgĩ wa Thiong'o, Kwesi Armah, and Tayeb Salih, among others.[17]

El-Salahi's career as an artist was suddenly interrupted in September 1975, when he was arrested, beaten, and imprisoned, falsely accused of anti-government activities. Released after six months in prison without trial, El-Salahi soon left Sudan and has since lived in exile, first in Doha and currently in Oxford, England. In his written memoir *Qabḍah min Turāb* (A fistful of earth), published in 2012, El-Salahi vividly describes life in Kober Prison as he experienced it, paying special attention to the daily routines of the prisoners and their interactions with prison and security officials, and beautifully interweaving this with reflections on his spirituality and Sufi ideals, through which he coped with the experience of unjust incarceration.[18] The *Prison Notebook* functions as a visual counterpart to the memoir, especially the section he dedicated to his experience in Kober Prison.

Unsurprisingly, El-Salahi's self-imposed exile has considerably affected the aesthetic orientation of his work. His early experimentation and his search for a new visual language have given way to a more philosophical orientation. Over the years, the somber colors of his earlier period and the brighter colors of the early 1970s have retreated to make way for a more assured exploration of aesthetic visions in black and white. The period following El-Salahi's incarceration, which he describes as a third phase in his artistic development, has been a stage of self-confidence and satisfaction, and the work reflects the accumulation of a life's experience. In the late 1990s he wrote, "I have started to see the meaning of things with more clarity than before. My thoughts are more organized and I have more mastery of the skill of painting. I am more concerned now with the internal structure of the work, which I prefer to express in black and white."[19] El-Salahi does not subscribe to the traditional Western distinction between painting and drawing, which associates color and shape with painting, and line with drawing. He has argued, "There is no painting without drawing and there is no shape without line. . . . In the end, all images can be reduced to lines." Hence, he prefers to describe his works in pen-and-ink on paper as "shades" in black and white.[20]

El-Salahi's *Prison Notebook* demonstrates both his mastery of drawing and his skillful painterly hand. The drawings it contains are among the finest examples of his post-prison period, in which his work has evolved into what he terms "open-ended, endless, organic growth painting."[21] It can take a monumental size, as in his large, nine-part drawing *The Inevitable*, of 1984–85 (now in the collection of the Herbert F. Johnson Museum of Art, at Cornell University). Like *The Inevitable*, his works are often accomplished piecemeal on paper, then framed as separate but structurally related units that, when assembled, together form one large, unified object.

As part of their overall composition, the drawings in the *Prison Notebook* contain Arabic prose and poetry composed by the artist. These writings are executed in El-Salahi's hybrid calligraphic style, which combines classical Arabic with the vernacular styles he learned as a child in Qur'anic schools, and it is possible to trace in them his earlier fascination with the rhythm and structure of Arabic calligraphy and letters. In this volume, page-by-page translations of the text in the *Prison Notebook* are accompanied by commentary by the artist, in which he discusses the images and writings and recounts his experience in Kober Prison.

Containing some of El-Salahi's most powerful artistic expressions, the *Prison Notebook* will no doubt consolidate the artist's place in a broader scene, but it also serves as a sobering reminder of the agony of integrity contravened. Through the work, the prisoner's overwhelming suffering is transformed into courageous forms of agency and empowerment, breaking the shackles of dominance and domination in the honorable toil for social justice.

Salah M. Hassan is the Goldwin Smith Professor and Director of the Institute of Comparative Modernities and Professor of African and African Diaspora Art History and Visual Culture, Cornell University, Ithaca, New York.

Notes

1. These memoirs and testimonials include Mubārak Aḥmad Ṣāliḥ, *Yawmīyāt Mu'taqal Siyāsī* (Diaries of a political prisoner) (Khartoum: al-Najm al-Fiḍḍī, 1987); Muḥammad Sa'īd al-Qaddāl, *Kūbar: Dhikrayāt Mu'taqal Siyāsī fī Sujūn al-Sūdān* (Kober: Memoirs of a political prisoner in Sudanese prisons) (Khartoum: International Publishing House, 1998); Khalīl Ilyās, *Kūbar Hāghin wa-al-Dhikrayāt fī Sujūn Ja'far Numayrī* (Kober Hagen and the memories of Gaafar Nimeiri's prisons) (Khartoum: International Publishing House, 2008); and 'Abd al-Qādir al-Rufā'ī, *Nahwa Mashrū' Waṭanī li-Munahāḍat al-ta'dhīb* (Toward a national project against torture in Sudan) (Khartoum: self-pub., 2008). Another is the famous open letter of February 29, 1990, written by Fārūq Muḥammad Ibrahīm al-Nūr, a former professor of biology at the University of Khartoum, who was arrested on November 30, 1989, and tortured in secret detention sites known as "ghost houses" for teaching the theory of evolution. Ibrahīm's open letter, sent to the president of Sudan, Omar al-Bashir, detailed his imprisonment and torture at the hands of the National Islamic Front regime and gave the names of those who subjected him to this ill treatment. He called for the investigation of such crimes and demanded his immediate release. In November 2000 he sent another letter to President al-Bashir, asking for a truth-and-reconciliation committee, a public apology, and prosecution of those who committed crimes of torture and human rights violations.
2. The American activist and prison abolitionist Angela Davis has described the contemporary prison as an institution deeply entrenched in a

penitentiary system designed, historically, as a place of reforming outcasts and criminals rather than punishing them—itself a modernist response to older, punitive systems. Ironically, as Davis points out in relation to the United States, a presumed democratic society, the penitentiary is a failed experiment and an institution of racial injustice, with well over two million behind bars, half of them African Americans or other minorities. See Davis, *Are Prisons Obsolete?* (New York: Seven Stories Press, 2003).

3. The title of El-Salahi's work is meant to evoke the famous *Prison Notebooks* of the Italian Marxist Antonio Gramsci (1891–1937), which he wrote during his incarceration in Italy by the Fascist regime of Benito Mussolini between 1929 and 1935. They were smuggled out of prison and published, posthumously, in the 1950s.
4. The name Kober, by which the prison is now known, was originally derived from Cooper, the surname of the first director general of prisons in Sudan during the British colonial period. Located in Khartoum North, near the bank of the Blue Nile, Kober Prison was built in the early 1900s. Other major prisons in Sudan are Shala, in Darfur, and Port Sudan, in the country's Red Sea Province. All three are known to have housed inmates persecuted for their presumed political activity, both those incarcerated for extended periods without trial or sentencing, in a typical use of Emergency Laws in Sudan, and those subjected to a trial and sentencing. (In this essay, the term *political prisoner* includes both categories.) Some of these prisons are more notorious than others for their harsh conditions and mistreatment of this population.
5. See Alessandra Comini, *Schiele in Prison* (Greenwich, Conn.: New York Graphic Society, 1973). A comparison of Egon Schiele's prison drawings and El-Salahi's *Prison Notebook* would be an interesting subject for a separate scholarly study.
6. W. J. Berridge, "The Frailties of Prisons in Postcolonial Sudan: From Rehabilitation to Retribution, 1956–1989," *Middle Eastern Studies* 52, no. 3 (2016): 385–401.
7. Abdullahi Ali Ibrahim, *Manichaean Delirium: Decolonizing the Judiciary and Islamic Renewal in Sudan, 1898–1985* (Leiden and Boston: Brill, 2008), 221–23.
8. Berridge, "Frailties of Prisons," 385.
9. Ibid., 385–86.
10. For the root causes of the civil war and the eventual partition of Sudan, I refer the reader to my essays "Sudan: The Tumultuous Road to Partition," in *Lines of Control: Partition as a Creative Space,* eds. Iftikhar Dadi and Hammad Nasar (Ithaca, N.Y.: Herbert F. Johnson Museum of Art, 2012), 37–47, and "Darfur and the Crisis of Governance in Sudan: A Left Perspective," *SAQ: South Atlantic Quarterly* 109, no. 1, special issue, "What Is Left of the Left? The Politics and Culture of Sudanese Marxism," ed. Rogaia Mustafa Abusharaf (Winter 2010): 95–116.
11. Berridge, "Frailties of Prisons," 386.
12. Ibid.
13. Political incarceration has a long history in Sudan, extending back to the colonial period. In the postcolonial period, it began to intensify as a phenomenon during the first military regime of General Ibrahim Abboud (1958–64), which was overthrown by a democratic revolution on October 21, 1964, rehabilitating a vibrant but short-lived parliamentary rule (1964–69).
14. Sudan is known to have one of the oldest, best organized, and most popular Communist parties in Africa and the Arab world. The Sudanese Communist Party was established in the mid-1940s as an offshoot of the Egyptian Marxist movement. It is known for its effective role in the development of a vibrant civil society in Sudan and the rise of a strong trade union movement, organizing among workers, peasants, women, and university students.
15. Besides authoring several works while in prison, Abdel Khaliq Mahgoub (1927–1971) also completed the translation of two books into Arabic: Hyman Levy and Helen Spaulding, *Literature for an Age of Science* (London: Methuen, 1952), which he translated in 1963 and first published in 1967 (repr. Khartoum: 'Azza Publishing House, 2008), and Joseph V. Stalin, *Marxism and Problems of Linguistics* (Moscow: Foreign Languages Publishing House, 1952), the translation of which was never published.
16. In Sudan, social relationships—such as kinship or familial ties—have been, and still are, exploited by prisoners' families to improve the conditions of prisoners' detention or secure their release. Prisoners' families put pressure on individuals in government to whom they have such a tie, essentially shaming them into using their power to mediate with the authorities to allow family visitations, access to medicine, or the release of the prisoner.
17. El-Salahi participated along with several other African writers and artists in the Mbari Club, an experimental arts and drama workshop in Ibadan, Nigeria, initiated by the German-British expatriate Ulli Beier and his British wife, Georgina Beier, a painter, in the late 1950s and early 1960s. Several Mbari Club members later emerged as great novelists, dramatists, and playwrights; their works have greatly impacted the growth of modern African arts and literature.
18. See El-Salahi, *Qabḍah min Turāb: Sīrah Dhātīyah* (A fistful of earth: A memoir) (Khartoum[?]: Muntadā Dāl al-Thaqāfī, 2012).
19. El-Salahi, correspondence with the author, 1998. The artist has reiterated this in several published interviews.
20. Ibid.
21. Ibid.

Translation of the *Prison Notebook* & Artist's Commentary

Ibrahim El-Salahi's *Prison Notebook* of 1976 is reproduced in its entirety in this volume. It begins on the last page of this book and is read from right to left, as is conventional for Arabic writings. The *Notebook*'s front cover serves as the back cover of this volume. A reproduction of the *Notebook*'s green paper jacket (likely a repurposed file folder added after the artworks were completed), it bears the printed commercial designations "Kent Super File" and *Mqāblāt*, an Arabic word meaning "Meetings."

An English translation of the *Notebook*'s Arabic text is accompanied here by page-by-page commentary about the work by the artist, recorded in Oxford, England, in November 2011.

IBRAHIM EL-SALAHI: I was released from Cooper Prison in March 1976, and months later I was still under house arrest. I just sat there . . . I could move around but only within limits. The experience I had been through, I wanted to record it. I have always been in the habit of jotting down whatever happens to me—I make notes. It had been a very bitter and also a rather enriching experience, in a strange way. So I started jotting it down in writing and drawing—the different images and the different places and the people I had met and what happened within those very, very high sandstone walls. You couldn't see anything except the sky and the kites flying, flying above . . . I started to record it so as not to forget. Not only for me but for anyone who is innocent and has been imprisoned under false pretenses. Just to remember what can happen.

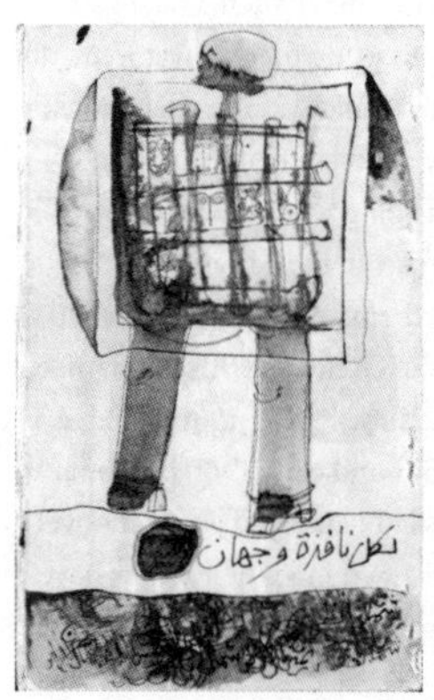

Each window has two faces.

I was arrested on the eighth of September. This drawing is a kind of figure, and in its chest is a jail. I gave it a title, because I mix writing and drawing. It says, "Each window has two faces." The internal face: who you were and what you were doing and your intentions and hopes and aspirations. And the outer face: It comes from beyond. You have no control over it, but it has control over you.

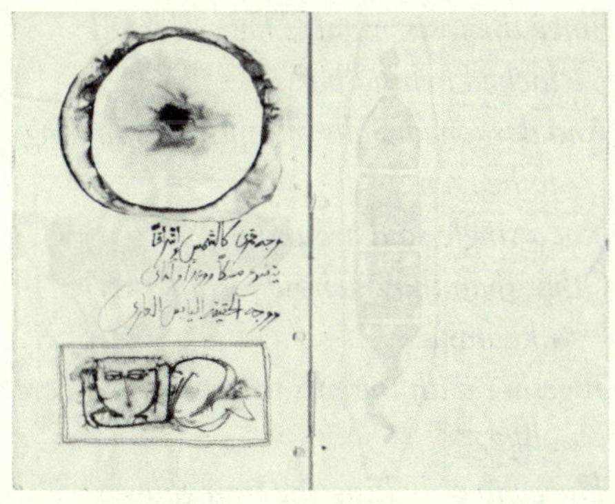

A moonlike face as bright as the sun
Diffusing musk, promises, and hopes,
And the bare face of truth.

This face shows how I used to understand people and how I thought about them. They appeared to me like a face, a moon face, very clear, very far away, aloof—but sympathetic. And that face can turn to give you another face to reality, and you are squeezed into nothingness. You become someone with no identity, not even a number.

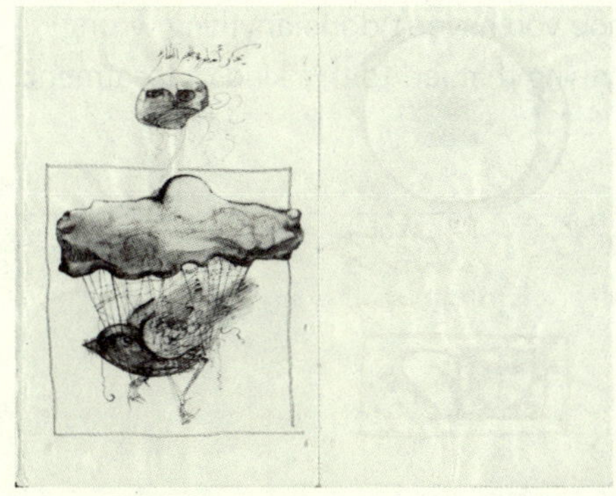

Recounting the myth of the flying stone

This is a strange thing. When you are ruled by people who have nothing but the weight of their power over you, you are subjected to something and not allowed to fly about like a free bird. Your freedom has been taken away from you and becomes like a huge rock that is going to destroy your world, and you can do nothing—not a thing—about it.

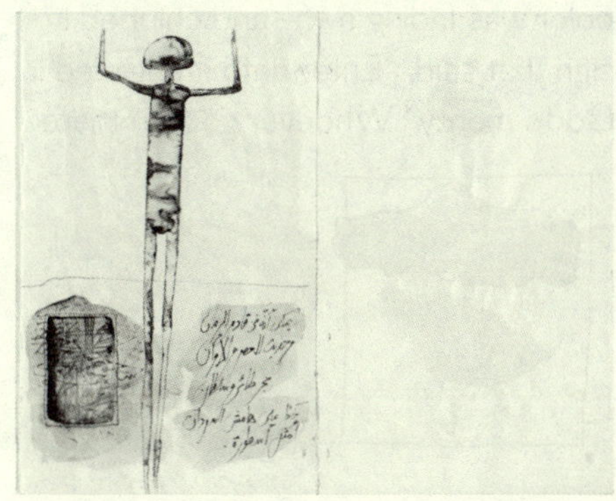

It was thus foretold that in a time yet to come,
The tale of what is here and now.
A flying rock and a sultan
Have engraved, at the peripheries of Sudan,
A perfect myth.

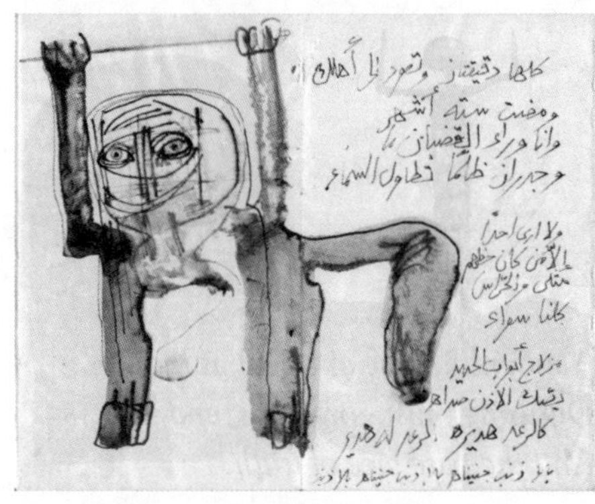

"It won't take more than a couple of
minutes
And you'll be back home safe and sound."

Since then, six months have elapsed
locked behind bars
And darkened walls of injustice spiraling
to heaven.
Not a single soul around,
Other than those whose fortunes were
like mine.
Together with the prison guards, we were
alike.
The echo of bolting the iron gates is
deafening,
Like thunder roaring, for no guilt of ours,
For no guilt of mine, for no guilt . . .

This says that here I was being kept. You can't go home, you can't see your children, you can't do anything at all. You are at their mercy, behind bars. And the very heavy metal doors shake your ears with a strong sound so that you can't hear anything at all. It's just like thunder. Since you haven't done anything wrong, you can't convince yourself that you did anything that led to this kind of treatment. It kind of keeps you in continuous shock.

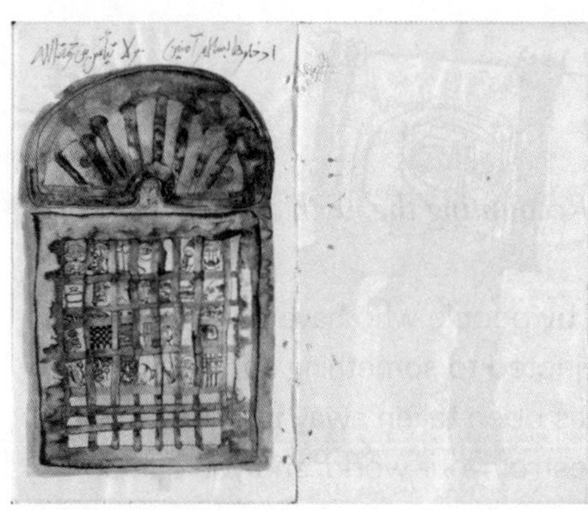

Enter unto it engulfed in peace and
security.
And do not despair of God's mercy.

This reminds me of the day I was taken to Cooper Prison and was faced with this gate—a huge gate. It was painted, but the color was fading away and chipped in certain spots. Above the gate there was a sign that said, "Enter unto it engulfed in peace and security. And do not despair of God's mercy." Whoever goes in there is already despairing of anything at all!

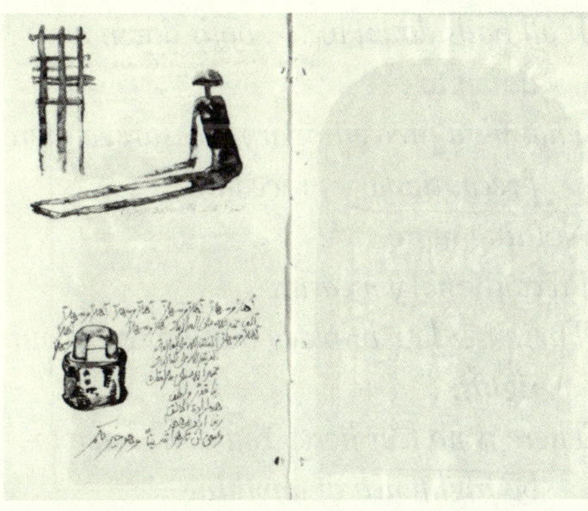

Welcome, welcome, welcome, welcome.
Thanks be to God you're safe and sound.
Welcome.

Thousands of thanks to Allah that you're back safe and sound.
Thousands of thanks to Allah that you're back safe and sound.
Our lord was merciful in what was destined.
This is our Creator's volition.
"But it may be that you dislike something while it is good for you."

This is about the time I went into the east-end cells and found the people who were sitting there, people whom I had missed for some time. I thought they had left the country or that they were no longer there—I found them inside. One of them was a professor of philosophy at the University of Khartoum; others were the minister of information, lawyers, and so forth. They said, "Thanks be to God you're safe and sound." I thought those political prisoners must have gone mad. How could they congratulate me on coming to this wretched jail? And they said, "Thousands of thanks to Allah that you're back safe and sound."

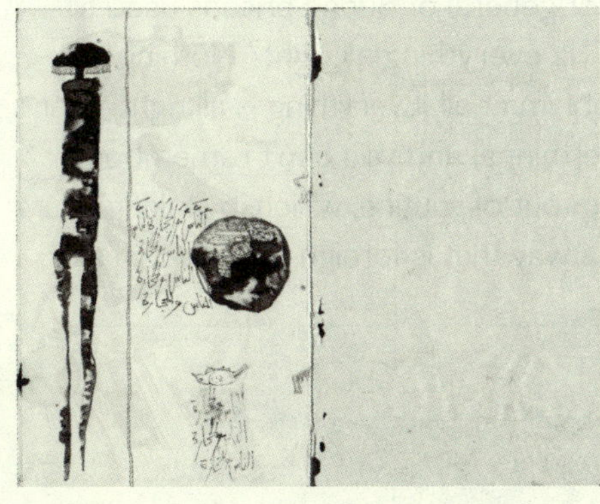

People and rocks
People and rocks
People and rocks
People and rocks

"People and rocks. People and rocks. People and rocks." I kept repeating this almost like a prayer, trying to see how in certain situations you can be petrified, you can become static. At the same time, you are a human being. You have a heart, you have a mind, you have a brain. You have an apparatus within you that can show you the right way and the wrong way, so you can maneuver your destiny as you go along. But sometimes it takes you back. By the actions of others, you are made into a stone to protect yourself, to protect your innocence. You petrify yourself because of the situation.

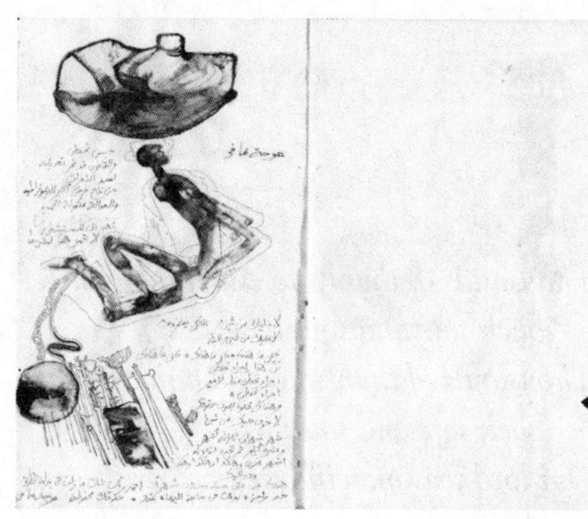

No problem.
You are to be kept in custody.
And the law has just been modified to get rid of any loopholes,
To make room for greater opportunities for democracy.
Justice is guaranteed to all people.
Feel at home.
Go to the hospital.
Don't worry at all.
There is nothing against you. Everybody knows that.
There is nothing against you at all.
It all boils down to . . . boils down to . . . down to . . .
That it's a precautionary measure, a mere precautionary procedure,
Nothing more.
Precautionary measure.
There is a law in place that protects your rights.
There is no fear here. You don't have to be frightened of anything.
Just a month, two months, three months
And ten days, and it will automatically be renewed for another three months
And ten days, and so on and so forth.
Some people had to stay behind bars for sixty-six months.
You should be thankful to Providence that you're still at the very beginning of the road.
Be relaxed. Your body needs to be relaxed. Stretch your body a little.
Your rights are sacred, protected. No problem whatsoever.

At the beginning of every month, the director general of Sudan prisons used to come to check in on us. He always asked, "Is everything all right? Nothing wrong?" And we all had to answer, "No problem at all. Everything is all right, your Excellency!" You hear yourself saying these things, and you can't remember your own voice because you are saying them out of routine, which, by taking your initiative from you, forces you into acting in a way that is foreign to your own self.

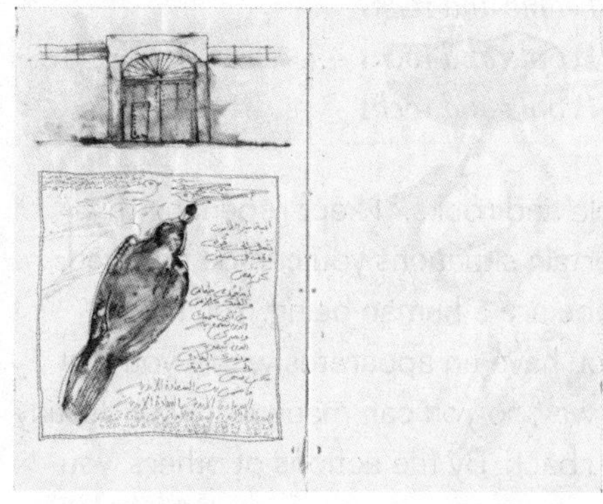

THE SONG OF THE TYRANT'S BIRD

Come close to me.
Stand by my side.
Keep me company.
I'll share my food with you.
I'll dictate my words unto you
Until I become the ears for your hearing,
Your eyes with which you know,
Your guiding light leading to my path.
Be with me. I guarantee you everlasting eternal happiness.
Eternal happiness, eternal happiness, eternal . . . eternal happiness . . .

I gave this bird the song of the bird of the devil, the governing devil.

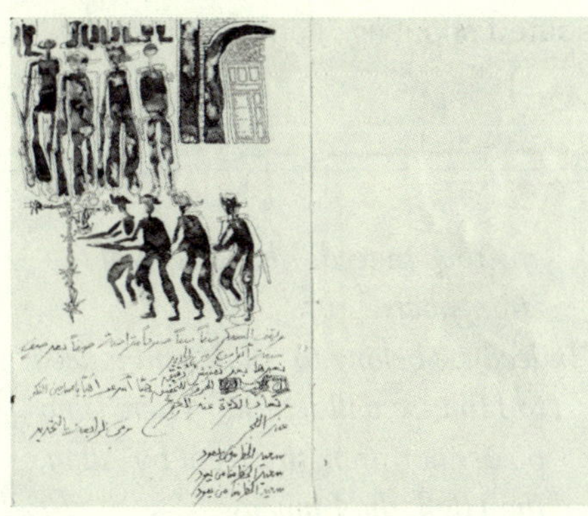

The soldiers line up row after row; in readiness they wait.
We cross through seven iron gates.
Subjected to a thorough and meticulous body search,
We are then allowed out to be escorted to interrogation.
Hurry up, hurry up, you prisoners of wretchedness.
The same ordeal is to be repeated on our way back to our cells.
At dawn, at the stroke of four,
Lucky is the one who would be brought back to jail.
Lucky is the one who would be brought back to jail.
Lucky is the one who would be brought back to jail.

This refers to the prison guards. Row after row of prison guards with weapons. Behind them, doors of steel. You cross through those doors after being searched—very, very meticulously searched. The prison guards are always asking you to hurry up. And the thing is repeated continuously. Happy are those who return.

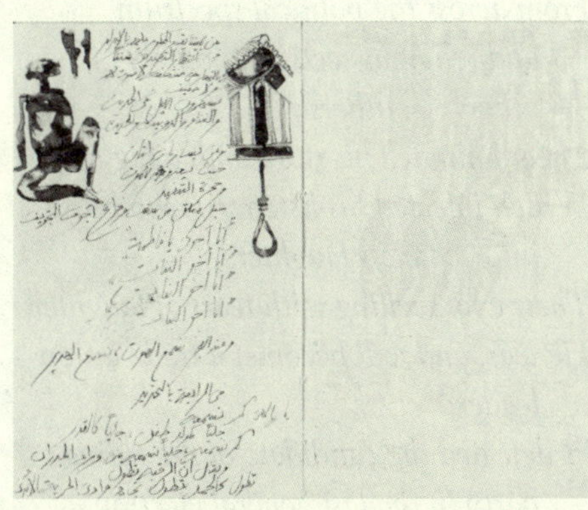

To our right languish those who are on death row,
Awaiting official approval of execution by hanging.
During the day, up to midday, they are engulfed in dead silence.
They go on chattering, singing, and reciting folk poetry all night long.
To our left, there were two desolate cells,
Where those sentenced to death were prepared for execution.
The gallows,
A rope hanging from the ceiling and a hollow cavity of emptiness:
"I am your brother, Fatima,
I'm the custodian of the clan's girls."
"I'm the custodian of the clan's girls."
"I'm the custodian of the clan's girls."
At dawn, we hear the voice, we hear the roaring.
At the stroke of four!
Oh my God, how clearly resonant that voice was.
It was as clear as the scream of a new-born baby, clear like destiny.
How many times we heard that voice from behind the thick walls.
It was said that the hanged neck stretches.
It stretches like that of a camel, stretches toward the valley of eternal freedom.

They would take a person in the afternoon and tie him with a *gulsheen* [puttee], soaked in salt water. At dawn, at four o'clock in the morning, you heard the trapdoor banging when the body, being heavy, dropped. But before that, you heard those who were about to be executed shouting "I am your brother, Fatima," to show that they were not afraid.

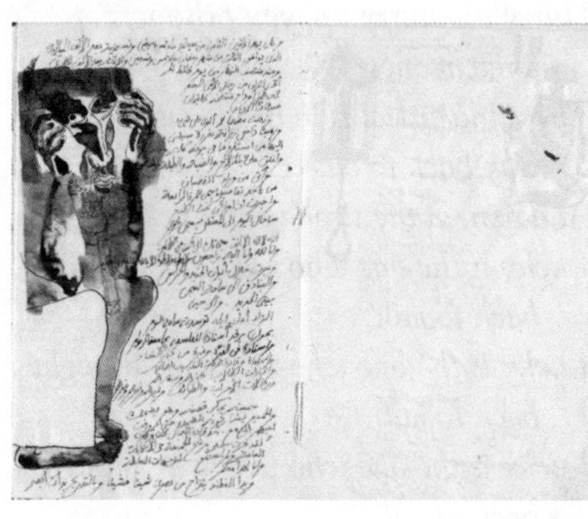

It was Monday, the eighth of September,
1975, corresponding to the third day
of Ramadan in the Hijri year 1395.
At swelteringly hot midday, they
came.
They were two General Security officers,
One of them with puffy cheeks,
Like dumplings prepared as alms for
dead wealthy people.
I, without much ado, went with them.
There, I was thrown into a single dun-
geon, already occupied
By someone who had thrown up the
contents of his stomach.
I was locked up behind securely bolted
iron gates.
Someone came from outside the iron bars,
For the fourth time that day, to take
down the details of my full name.
I was told then that the procedure was
underway.
They were typing the papers.
I was to be transferred that day to the
detention center at Kober (Cooper)
Prison.
"There is no deity except You; exalted
are You. Indeed, I have been of the
wrongdoers."
"Indeed we belong to Allah, and indeed
to Him we will return." There is no
power nor strength except by Allah,
the High, the Immense.
I walked in through the massive iron
gates, guards,
And guns, into the prison yard.
My temporary new home.
I slept rough on the bare floor the first
night,
Alongside a Khartoum University
philosophy professor,
A lecturer in nuclear physics, among
high-ranking judges,
Advocates, trade and student union
leaders, political activists
From across the political spectrum
and religious sects, and others . . .
others . . . others . . .
I heard him tell his story with a big laugh,
Which infected his listeners, who burst
into ceaseless laughter,
Their eyes welling with tears of laughter.
He was, and will become, a trade union
leader:
"I defeated the candidate of the ruling
party in the last general election.
I didn't heed the instructions and direc-
tives of the regime.
That is why I was thrown into jail."
Then, gradually, the thin layer of foggy
ignorance started to be lifted from
my mind's eye,
And I began to perceive the true essence
of things.

I remember they said, "Now that your papers are signed, you are being taken to jail." At that moment you become numb, because of the shock of what is happening to you. You don't know what to say, you don't know what to think. This is something that just fell out of the sky onto your head—*bang*—and you have to . . . There's nothing you can do.

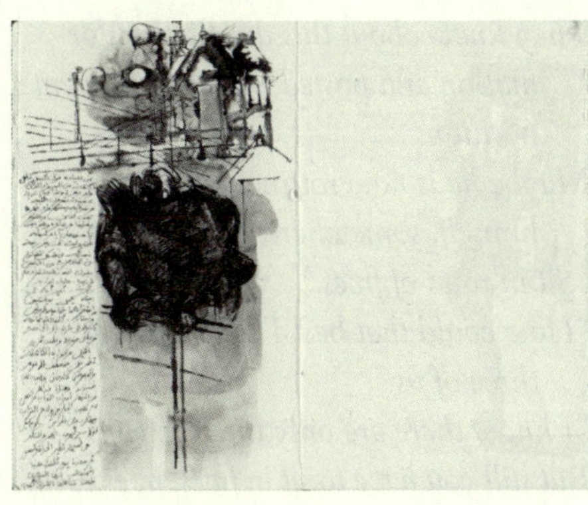

From his lofty position on top of the prison wall,
We could see his massive darkish body overlooking us.
He was born in Ghazza and brought up in the Nuba Mountains.
He carries twenty bullets and a rifle, slung behind his back.
He cherishes the songs of Umm Kulthum.
He used to sing her songs with exhalations and sighs.
He lamented the days of his bygone youth.
We used to ask him to describe how the streets,
The people, and the buses on the roads looked.
He would grumblingly retort, saying he wanted to buy sugar,
But it was nowhere to be found on sale.
He wanted to get matches and gasoline for lanterns.
But to no avail.
He ended up buying two eggs for eight piastres and was left bewildered.
He had eight children, the eldest of whom was ready to go to college.
He used to go on singing and we kept asking for more.
During the long, boring evenings, searchlights
Flooded all corners of the prison yard.
Sleepless, and maddened by the ceaseless buzzing of swarms of mosquitoes
Sucking our blood.
During the day, the army of ants and swarms of flies,
Joining forces with the hellish day heat and sandstorms,
Endlessly assail and benumb the senses.
If not for the patience of Job on our part,
Trepidation and sullenness.
High above in the sky the kite bird and vultures flew.
We were over the moon the day a little dove stopped by.
We rejoiced in the presence of that bird of good tidings.

I remember that one prison guard, one of those at the top of the wall, used to sing. He used to live in Egypt; he's from the Nuba Mountains. Very, very, very dark in complexion. He used to sing the songs of Umm Kulthum, the famous Egyptian singer. And we loved that, because it was really something. Just imagine a guard with a machine gun on top of railings with floodlights, singing beautiful songs about love, about hope, about human beings, about freedom, about this and that. The days when he was not on duty we missed him enormously.

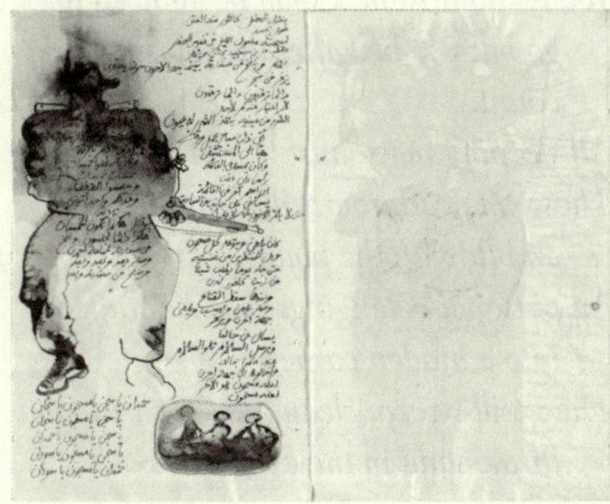

Hulking, with the throat of an ox
And the body of a giant.
His complexion had the impact of pitch-dark nights on the hearts of little children.
With a perpetually frowning forehead,
Rebuking and scolding prisoners.
Blowing his whistle, while others circle around us to take the daily morning count.

Heavily breathing in utter weariness, he hollers,
"Forever and a day, lazily you lie down doing nothing,
With no consideration for anybody,"
Sparks of fury emitted from bloodshot eyes.
One morning he came, a paper in his hand, and howled,
"Get up, let us go to the hospital."
He was holding the list of names upside down.
He dragged me aside to ask about the next name on the list,
To conceal his illiteracy.
He used to curse and threaten every prisoner.
Woe to those waiting on death row if he was enraged.
Until one of those days he asked me for a favor.
He wanted a little of the camphor oil I had then.
The mask of heartlessness had finally fallen.
He went on cursing, insulting, and threatening prisoners in other sections,
Sparing us the ordeal of his curses.
Instead, he started sending his greetings.
They knew about this drastic transformation and posted him to a different position.
Maybe he is now rotting, a prisoner himself, somewhere.
"Sit in rows of fives."
"How could that be? There are only three of us."
"I know there are only three of you,
But still you have to sit in fives, fives each."
The three of them squatted on the ground.
He went on to count, "One, two, three," then retorted,
"That is how to sit in fives,
This is how you should line up every morning,"
Blowing his whistle to draw the attention of another group of prisoners.
He went on counting and counting,
Blowing his whistle, then count and count and count.
Oh Hamdan, you are a prison, a prisoner, and a prison guard.
Ye, a prison, a prisoner, a prison guard.
A prison, a prisoner ye, Hamdan.
Ye, a prison, a prisoner. Oh Sudan.
Hamdan, a prisoner in Sudan.

This is about one of the prison guards who was responsible for our cells. His name was Hamdan. I think he came from western Sudan. He was very strong, like a bull. He came many times at dawn, at five in the morning, to wake the prisoners and make them sit in groups of five. And he would count. I didn't know that he couldn't read or write until the day he came with a piece of paper and he was holding it upside down. This is about him, about the prison, and about Sudan. Because what was happening to him, what was happening to us—we were all in a big prison.

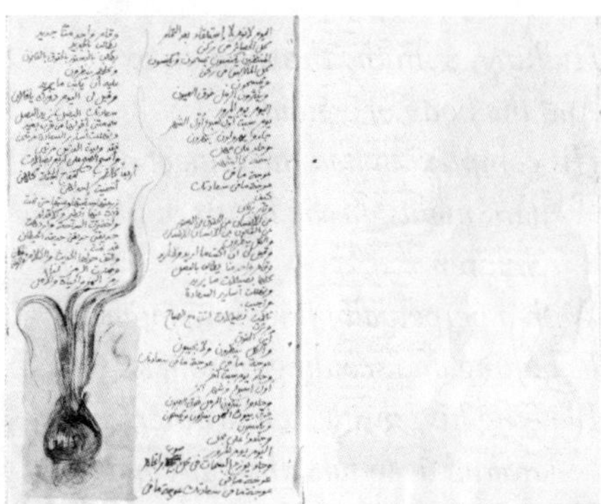

Today, no prisoners shall be allowed to go back to bed after the morning count.
All sleeping mats must be put away.
Those on death row will clean, sweep, and tidy up the place.
All personal belongings shall be stuffed into a hidden corner.
They will sweep, clean, sweep clean, and throw sand in the eyes.

Today is the day for the inspection round.
The first Saturday of the first week of every month.
They rushed in, hollering and scolding everyone.
Then he leisurely walked into the place with a big smile.
"No problem at all. Everything is all right, your Excellency!"
How come? I was fuming with rage!
What about the human in us, what about rights and the constitution?
What about law enforcement and humans, humanity?
Everybody was looking apprehensive.
I was told to put my demands and objections in writing.
One of us stood up and demanded a provision of onions!
The Excellency's face radiated with exhilaration.
The demand was answered.
Three little onions were brought into the prison the next morning.
I was infuriated.
What about our rights?
All prison mates were speechlessly gazing at me.
"No problem. Everything is all right, your Excellency."
And another first Saturday of the first week of the month arrived.
The death row inmates came in once more, throwing sand in the eyes.
Throwing sand on anthills, scrubbing and cleaning.
They hurriedly came in.
The day is inspection day.
He came in, at his leisure, with unabashed smiles in all directions.
"No problem. Everything is all right, your Excellency. No problem."
A different inmate stood up to the occasion this time, with new demands.
Demanding enforcement of constitutional rights, law enforcement and order.
All were gazing apprehensively, speechless.
"You have to write down what you ask for."
Then I was told that it was my turn to put forward our demands.
"Your Excellency, the onions, we want onions."
I heard myself repeating that from a distant nearness.
Once more, the face of the Excellency radiated with exhilaration.
I have learned my lesson twice.
The next morning four onions were brought in,
Four beautiful moonlike onions, like paradise apples.
I hid away one of these onions.
I planted, watered, and took care of that onion.
It grew up a lush green plant.
I kept fending off birds and feet from my little garden.
The prison yard turned flourishing green.
My garden, the garden, the garden of walls, was in full bloom.
It was there and then the favorite subject for our chatter.
A symbol for all of us, for growth, life, and hope.

This one has a long story. I mentioned earlier that the prison director used to come once a month to check on us. He would ask us if anything was wrong. "No problem at all. Everything is all right, your Excellency!" After he checked on us and we answered him and assured him that everything was all right, nothing was wrong at all, he would ask, "Do you need anything?" One of us, someone I knew very well indeed, was a political activist. He said, "Your Excellency, can we have some onions?" The food was inedible; in the morning we had broad beans that were very old, without salt or oil, nothing. For the first few days I didn't eat at all. I just left it for other prisoners who were too hungry to refuse.

Putting onions near your nose made it easier for you to swallow the food. Just imagine. These were political prisoners from the so-called elite of the country. When the director and all the other people from the prison and security left, I went to my friend and said to him, "You call yourself a political activist and all you ask for is onions? What about freedom? What about the constitution? What about the rights of human beings and so on?" He didn't say anything. Then he said, "Next month it is your turn to ask for the onions." I said, "What?" He said, "Next time it will be your turn, because we all depend on these onions."

The next morning the prison guard who was responsible for our cells brought three onions. And everyone was very happy. A month passed and the time came when I was supposed to ask for the onions. He came and asked, "Nothing wrong?" "Everything is all right, your Excellency." He looked here and there and then asked, "Do you need anything?" I could not make myself ask for the onions. I thought it was too low, the sort of thing that would take away everything in you that you thought was human. He kept looking at me because he knew that it was my turn to ask for the onions. I couldn't hear my voice when I said, "Your Excellency, the onions, we want onions." I barely managed to get it out. The prison director was very happy to see that this Undersecretary of Something had been brought down to ask for onions, so everything must be working fine.

The next morning, the prison guard brought four onions as a kind of honoring of the Undersecretary's request. One of the onions had two segments, so I gave three and a half onions to the person in charge of the mess, of the food provisions for the cells for the whole month, and I kept one segment of the onion. At that time I was responsible for the water, for the drinking jar, which was a big terra-cotta jar that I had to fill with water. What dripped from it made a bit of a muddy pool underneath. I planted the onion in the sandy ground and kept taking care of it, telling people not to step on it, please! I just wanted to see something green, because the earth was covered with sand, and the walls were sandstone, and you couldn't see anything except the blank sky above with the kites flying. When it started growing, I used to sit for hours watching this onion getting green and sprouting. The prisoners used to come one by one and sit beside me to watch this onion! They called it Salahi's Garden.

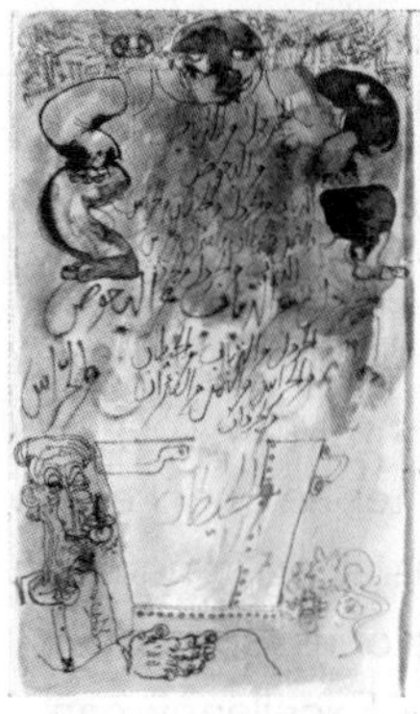

The defecation bucket and flies
And mosquitoes

The flies and the bucket and prison walls
and prison guards
Ants, prison walls, and mice and prison
guards
The flies, defecation bucket, and rats
Defecation bucket, the flies, and
mosquitoes
Defecation bucket, the flies, and the
prison walls
The prison guards, ants, and mice,
And rats, guards, rats, walls, mice

In the cell, there were ten of us. Packed like sardines. On the concrete floor. No beds, no mattresses, nothing. Each of us was given just a blanket and nothing else. I remember next to the cell there was a bucket that was always flowing toward us. It was terrible.

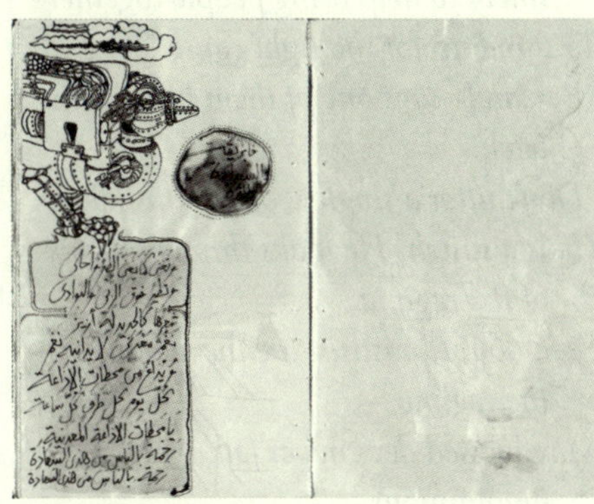

FLYING HAPPINESS FACTORY

You sing more sweetly than birds.
You fly over hillocks and grasslands.
With ironlike humming lyrics,
An unmatched metallic melody
Broadcast from radio stations,
Every single morning, every hour.
Oh, metallic radio stations,
Have mercy on people and spare them such cruel happiness.
Spare them such cruel happiness.

This is about the propaganda that was spread all over the country through broadcasting. I wrote that this propaganda sounded like a bird, with its very sweet song.

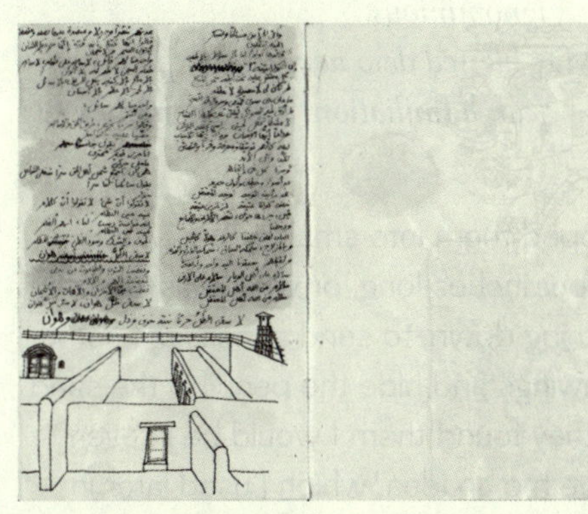

The prison guards came,
High-ranking officers and the low rank and file:
"Today you are to be transferred."
Brusquely, they spluttered their instructions,
Allowing no questions or requests.
"To the Quarantine Section A you shall leave.
Take all your belongings under your armpit."
I had neither a sleeping mat nor a bed cover,
Nothing other than what I was wearing then: a dirty shirt and a pair of pants.
I didn't brush my teeth last night or this morning.
I didn't even have a comb to tidy up my unkempt beard.
My hair was soiled with sand.
Good-bye dear ones, good-bye dears.
It was a night of warm intimacy and understanding
That we spent together.
Now it is over once and for all.
We left, each on a different route,
Through wall after wall in the maze of the prison iron gates.
I have seen the face! The face of detention,
Behind ancient apertures in ancient prison dungeons.
It was reported, impoverished rats in these cells bite human limbs and figures.
And we entered.
The iron gate locked behind our backs, with a menacing roar, like a mountain,

Its bolt as thick as an arm's or leg's length.
There were four and one detainees
already there.
Peace be upon the dwellers of this place,
peace be on earth.
God's peace be upon you, dwellers of this
detention hole.
God's peace be upon you, dwellers of this
detention hole.
Their meager belongings: nothing more
than sleeping mats,
A defecation bucket, a small table with a
single onion on top of it.
They told us it was a rare gem, with
magical powers,
An antidote against poison and sorrows.
One of us told them to finish off their
meal first.
Prison food was tasteless, colorless, lacking in salt and spices,
With no gravy, no meat, no bone, not
even teeth.
One of us inquired, "Who are you?"
"We are members of the Liberation
Party," they said.
"The Truthful Path, we firmly adhere to
Islam."
The fifth of them retorted, "I'm an old
hand, a tempered political activist.
Working-class activist, working clandestinely to help bring people together
To stand up for the right cause."
"Beware!" says one of them behind his
back.
"Don't utter a single word to this fellow.
He is a snitch. He looks through the eyes
of the regime.
Fear, doubt, mistrust are the canons of
the regime."
May blessed dew never fall upon the
ignominious.
I have shaken off tyranny and despotism
from my soul.
I have shaken off worry and pain,
Shaken off sorrows, laments, and
trepidation.
May blessed dew never fall upon the
ignominious.
May blessed dew never water plants of
fear, humiliation, and ignominy.

I had some cement-bag casings, and I chopped them into small pieces. And there was a pencil. One little pencil about four inches long, or what was left of it. We used it to write something or jot something down, to send a message somewhere. I remember I used to make little drawings and hide the pencil in the sand and also hide the small papers, because if they found them I would be in even more trouble than I was in already. That gave me an idea, which I used later in my work: the organic growth of a picture. I used to make very tiny drawings on these little pieces of paper that I buried in the sand after finishing them. I worked on a nucleus, something in the middle. Then I added one piece to the right, then one piece to the left, one piece above, one piece below, until the picture grew into another image.

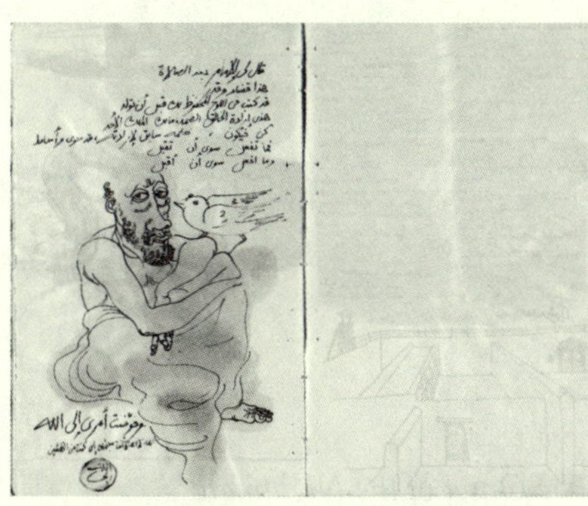

The imam said to me, after the prayers,
"It is divine providence."
Everything is entered unto your destined
Sacred Book before you are born.

It is the will of our Creator, the Eternal Refuge, Owner of Sovereignty, and the One and Only.
When He intends a thing that He says to it, "Be," and it is.
His knowledge precedes His will. He has encompassed all things in knowledge.
So you're left with nothing other than to surrender to His will.
I have but to surrender to His will.
I entrust my affair to Allah.
"There is no deity except You; exalted are You. Indeed, I have been of the wrongdoers."
He is Allah, my Lord.

The bird here is almost like my conscience, reminding me of what should be done.

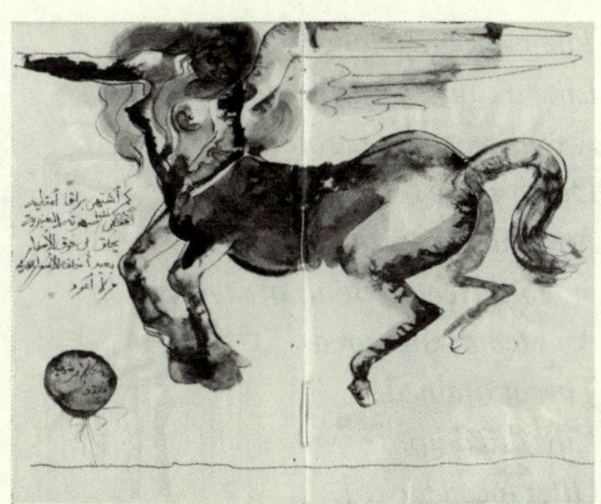

I yearn for a ride on the back of a Buraq.
Immersed I would be, in the ecstasy of its amber-colored horseback,
Soaring over far skies,
Far away from prison walls,
Never to return.

This is about how I wished to have a Buraq, which is a flying horse or donkey, or something in between. I would be engulfed in its amber perfume, and it would fly me over the walls, the thick walls of jail, and I would never return.

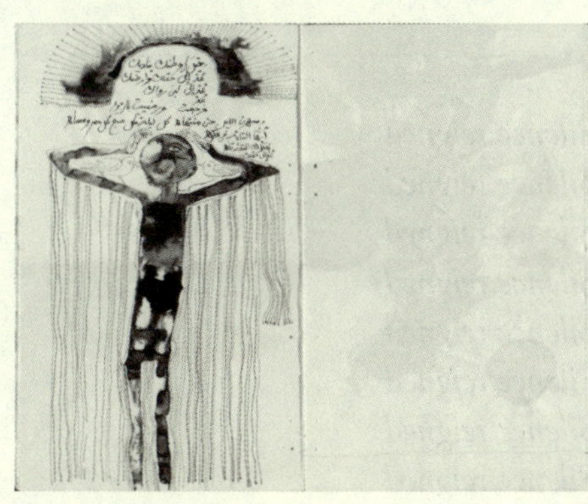

Your country is calling out for you,
I was told.

Go back to your field and land,
To the milk that quenched your thirst,
Go back.
I did go back,
Contentedly.
I stayed awake all night long,
Every night, every morning, afternoon, and evening.
Oh you who is lost in thoughts,
Your thoughts have gone astray.
Go back to your field.

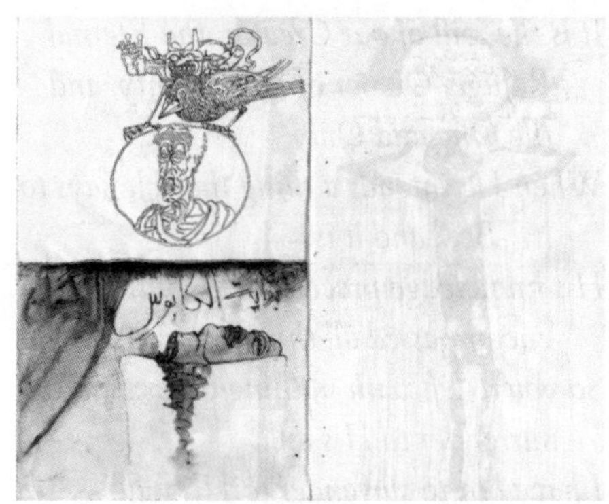

The Onset of the Nightmare

A bird of evil hangs over your head continuously and reminds you that you will be caught, you will be taken again. It repeats the bitter experience you have been through and the worries you have. It is a terrible situation. That was the beginning of the nightmare I used to have. When I was released at last, every single night I woke up from these horrible dreams. That is what made me start making small sketches, small abstract works in full color.

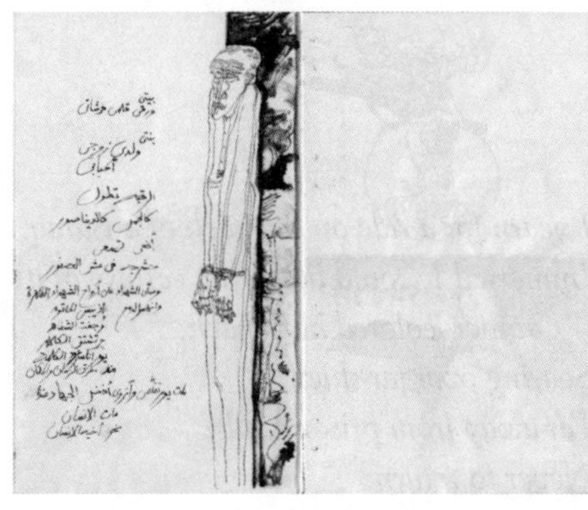

The neck grew longer,
Like a camel's, a dinosaur's.
A python coiling around
Death rattle on a bird's nest
And the martyrs offered prayers
to the chaste souls of martyrs.
And tears outpoured.
Throat drained.
Lips dried up.
Utterance cracked.
When the word's stake broke
At the cross point of time and place,
When we lost the drive to fight our
internal weaknesses,
Man died.
He slaughtered his own brother.

My home
My papers, pen, brush
My daughter
My son, my wife
My friends

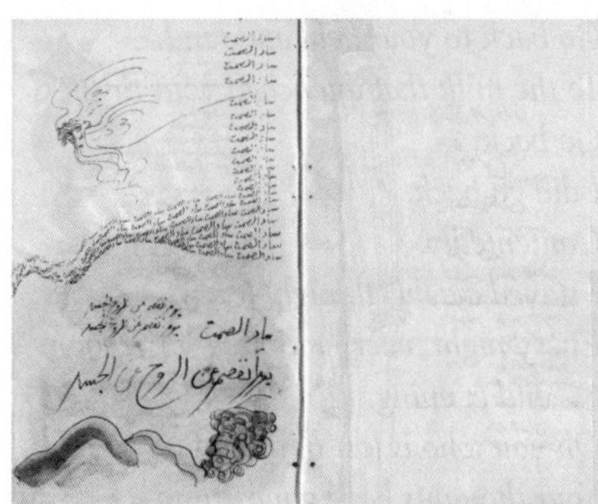

Silence reigned
Silence reigned
Silence reigned
Silence reigned
Silence reigned
Silence reigned
Silence reigned
Silence reigned
Silence reigned
When the body split from the soul
When the body split from the soul
When the body split from the soul

This is a repetition of the same phrase. Silence spread everywhere because nothing made sense. This was also in the nightmares I had, that silence spread everywhere on the day when the spirit was separated from the body.

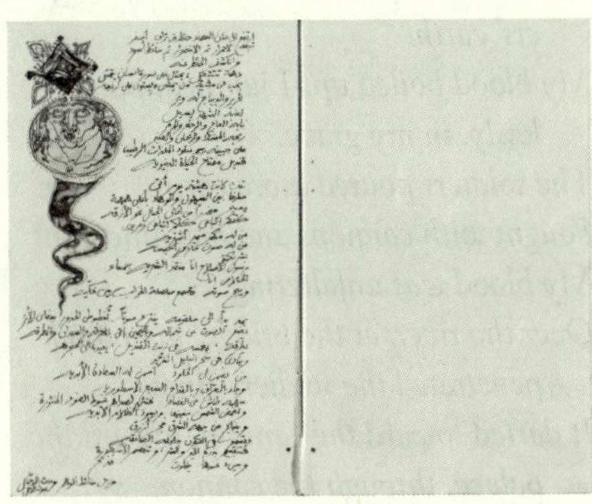

A wall of yellow dust soared to the sky,
Followed by redness, greenness, then a black wall.
The wall exposed a figure,
A black mass evolving, disguised in a human form,
Trotting and straightening as if four legged.
His apparel is a silk garment.
Honey is dripping out of his mouth.
His canine is of ivory, marble, and alabaster.
He smells of musk, basil, and ambergris.
His forehead depicts the dewy cluster of pleasures,
The light, the key to earthly life.
That was how he looked the day he came,
Yelling across plains and valleys,
Gliding down from mountaintops into alleyways:
You are my followers and disciples.
Whoever has a consciousness, I will buy it.
Whoever has a different voice, I will lock him up.
You can rejoice!
I am the messenger of reform, the savior of mankind!
I am redemption!
His voice became husky; the rattle of destruction could be heard between his jaws.
He extends a hand to his throat and pulls out a voice with octopus tentacles, of a diabolical nature.
He puts the voice to his left, and with his right hand he takes a burner, an anvil, and a hammer.
He hammers it, soaks it in the lantern oil, puts it back in his throat,
And calls out in a fancy voice, like that of an enchanting nightingale:
Whoever grants me immortality, I shall bestow him with eternal bliss.
He called in the soothsayer and the seven mythical goblets.
His arrow missed its mark and went too wide into space, its echo causing moaning among the scattered threads of light.
The sun closed its eyes, and darkness reigned in eternity.
From the east, a blue dawn broke,
A thunderbolt roared out loud in the universe,
The seed of goodness and evil split apart, and the myth disintegrated.
At that point death was brought forth to be slaughtered.
The wall of illusion was no longer there,
And the false prophet died once charlatanry died.

This represents the tyrant who ruled at the time, and how he tried to deceive the people and had to appear to them. On his forehead is the symbol of desire, the key to everlasting life. This is what I had been warned about when the prisoners said to me, "Thank God you are free."

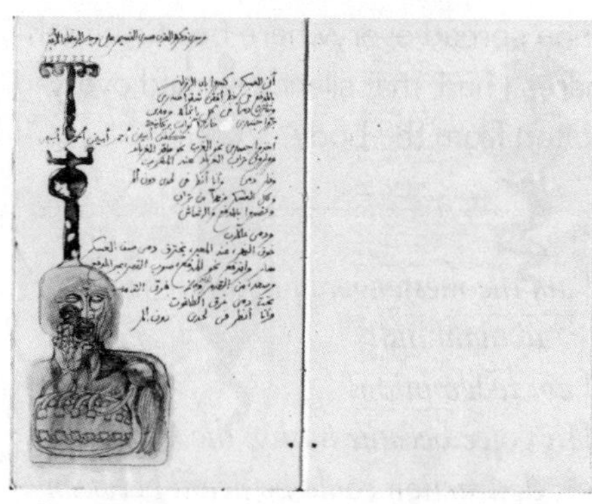

His sweet memory flew like a breeze on the dusty face of the heat.
The soldiers came, broke the cell's door.
With their cannon, they split open my chest in a horizontal line.
My blood sprinkled in every direction and every horizon.
They dragged my body through volcanic doors,
My shroud was white, red, white, red, white.
They took my body westward to the foreigners' cemetery.
At sunset, they buried me in the foreigners' earth.
My blood boiled up; I jumped, painlessly, in my grave.
The soldiers poured more earth,
Fought with cannons and machine guns.
My blood was unfaltering.
Over the river, at the bridge, my blood penetrated the soldiers' lines.
It darted toward the cannon, toward the palace, through the cannon.
It rose from bare feet to the top.
In my blood, tyranny drowned.
As in my grave, I painlessly watched.

This is what used to worry me enormously. These kinds of images of torture, of death, of blood, of earth, of being buried, of not being resurrected but getting out and moving, to fight as if my blood was going to take revenge on them.

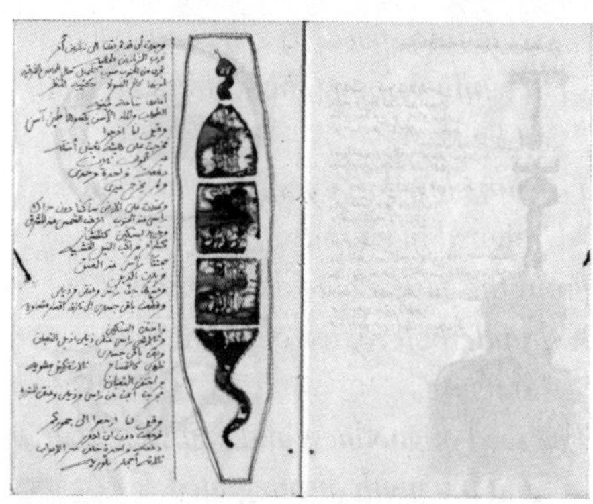

I realized that we had been moved to different cells
To the west of where we were kept for a while.
They ran from south to north, like the eastern cells.
They were grim, black, bleak, and ugly.
In front of them extended a clay court,
Littered with fungi and stinky water and clad with smelly clay.
They ordered us to come out.
I came out in the form of a python
Through three doors at once.
I came out alone.
No one else.
I lay on the ground, motionless,
My head to the south, anticipating
The sunrise in the east.
A saw-shaped knife was brought,
Like the mast of a wooden boat on the Nile.
My head was chopped off from the neck,
And my python tail was cut off.
When my head, neck, and tail went dry,
The rest of my body was cut into three equal portions.
Then the knife disappeared
And my head, neck, and tail, the python's tail, vanished,
But the rest of my body remained.

My back was like that of a crocodile:
three roasted blocks of flesh.
The snake disappeared,
And I ran about looking for my head,
my tail, and my chopped neck.

They ordered us to go back to our
burrows.
Without turning back, I returned, in one
breath, through the doors,
Three crystal stones.

I felt that I was lying down like a boa. And this boa was chopped into three parts. I was left there, and someone told me to put together those parts that had been cut off and go back into my hole. This is a reflection on the jail and the cell, on being tortured. You are torn apart.

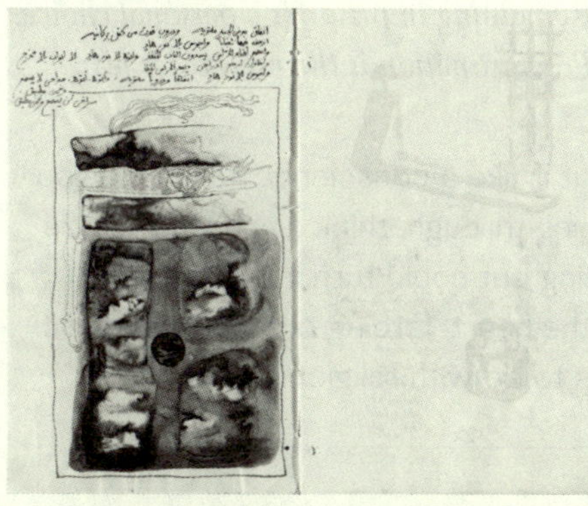

Tunnels, just wide enough for the body
to squeeze into, twisted and tight,
Routes carved of volcanic rocks.

I crawl through them, prowling blindly.
I hear the footsteps of guards, blocking
the only exit.
No guiding light, no exits, no way out,
I try to go back but the guards are up at
the gate.
I prowl blindly
Through twisted tunnels and routes.
I am lost.
My screams reach no one,
My mouth shut.
My screams will reach no one so long as
my mouth is shut.

Here I was remembering a nightmare where I was trying to go through some underground tunnels. I moved about, and whenever I found an outlet, the guards would close it. So I had to go backward through a very, very narrow hole. It made me feel claustrophobic, going back into these twisted lanes underground.

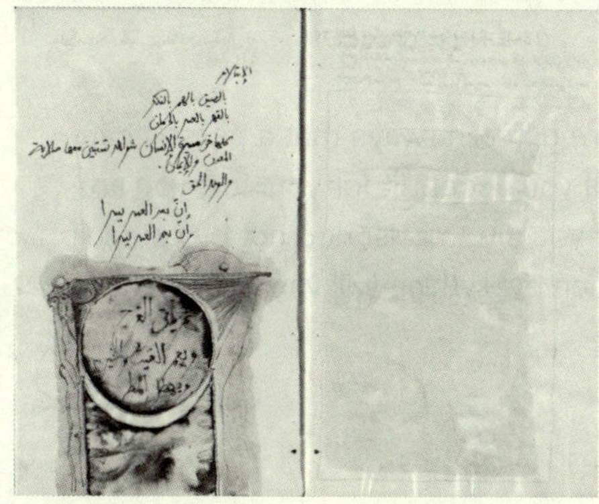

Affliction
By distress, grief, and petulance,
By coercion, hardship, and want
Are all tests of one's rigor and faith,
And belief in the sacrosanct promise
With hardship comes ease,
With hardship comes ease.

This has to do with difficult days. No matter how long they are, a time will come when things will be different. The Qur'an says, "With hardship comes ease."

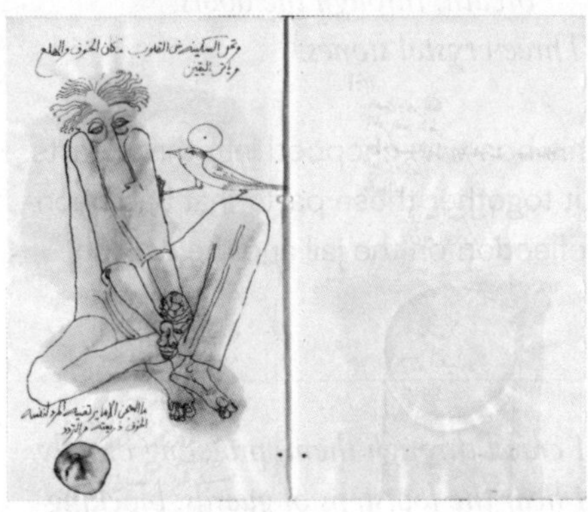

And peace will permeate the heart,
Forcing out fear and panic,
And unswerving faith will settle in.
Remaining in prison is a personal choice.
Procrastination is the pretext for fear.

This bird is a sign of hope. But sometimes it is like a conscience, talking to you. It tells you that whatever you have been going through, think again, and realize that there are things that appear as one thing but could turn into something else. This says, "And peace will permeate the heart, forcing out fear and panic, and unswerving faith will settle in." This has to do with religion.

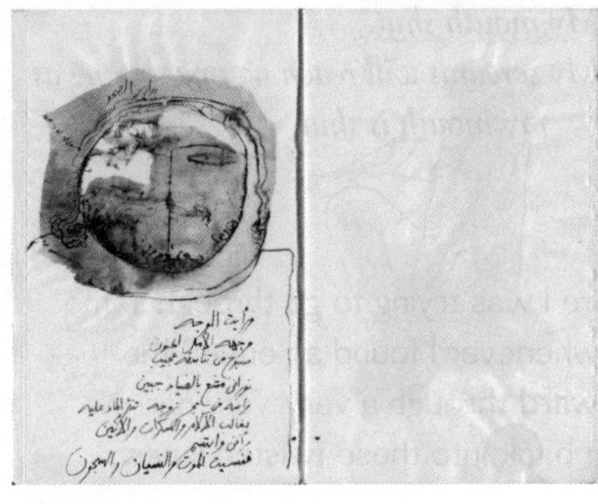

And I saw the face,
Beaming with warmhearted hope,
Luminous, in perfect proportions,
Radiant forehead,
His head on his wife's lap,
Sprinkling water on his head.
Despite his agony, writhing in the throes of death,
He smiled when he saw me.
I forgot all about death, obliviousness, and incarceration.

Jail is what is accepted by oneself. There are different ways that a person can accept what is happening to him or to her. If you accept it for yourself, you are imprisoning yourself. But you can be free. If you are imprisoned not by yourself but by other people, there will be a time when everything will vanish.

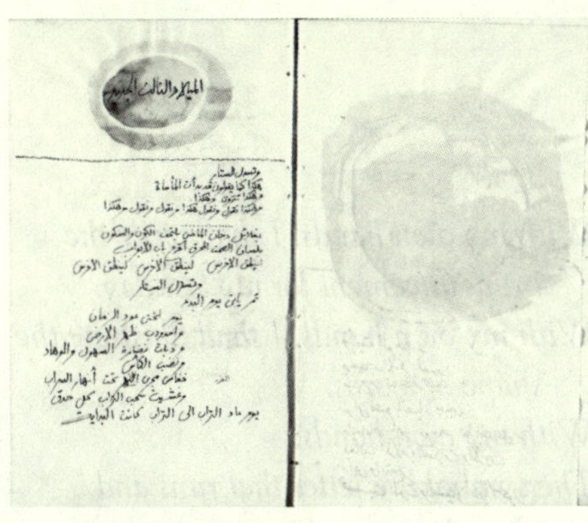

THE THIRD BIRTH

The curtains are drawn.
Thus, as the saying goes, the tragedy has
begun to unfold.
Thus, you retire, and thus,
Thus, we say, we say thus, we say and
say and thus . . .

In the smoke blanket of the past, the
universe is engulfed.
With the tongue of the burning silence,
I knock on the door of doors.
Let the mute speak up. Let the mute
speak up,
And the curtains are drawn.
Then the day of the beginning comes
When time's spine bent,
The earth's surface hunched,
The plains and ravines lost their bloom,
The glass was emptied.
The river course sank under the mirage
rivers,
And dust clouds invaded all eyes.
The day when "ashes to ashes" returned,
that was the beginning.

This is called "The Third Birth." It is about what happened after I was released from jail. It is a poem, and these are very complicated words, because I'm trying to talk about how things start and how things end and what happens in between. The process of change and movement and suffering, whatever happens to us in our world, goes on for some time but has to have an end. Every beginning has to have an end.

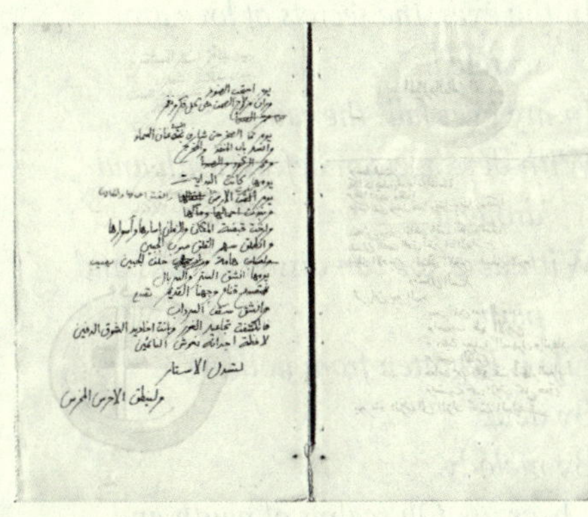

When light was veiled,
And the latch of silence reigned over
thought and melody,
When rock sprouted to the sky,
And the exit door was blocked,
That day was the beginning.
It was when the earth erupted and
discharged its burdens,

When place and time loosened their grip
on things,
And the uncertainty arrow darted toward
the forehead,
And hit a head behind the forehead.
On that day, all disguises and veils were
torn,
Our old face mask cracked,
The vault ceiling fractured,
The wrinkles of the innermost depths
were exposed,
As were the groves of the long-buried
longing,
The graves threw up the coffins of the
sleepers.
Let the curtains go down.
Let the mute, the muffled speak up.

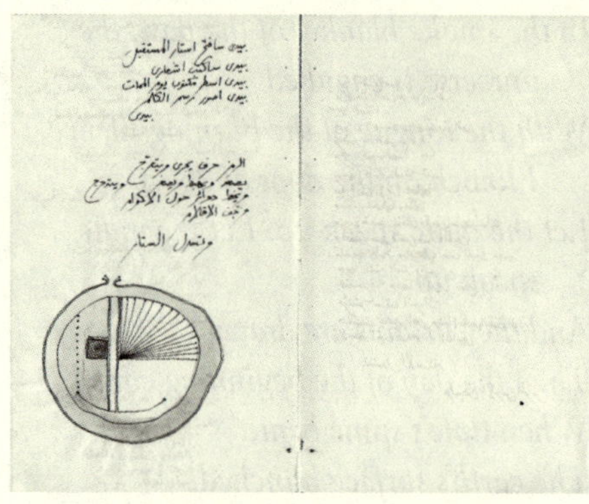

With my own hands, I shall open the
future's curtains.
With my own hands, I shall write my
poems.

With my own hands, I shall write the
pronouncement for my last day.
With my own hands, I shall illustrate the
shape of words.
With my own hands.
The symbol is a letter that runs and
meanders,
Going up and down, waning, rolling,
Making circles around piles.
And the pens run dry,
And the curtains are up.

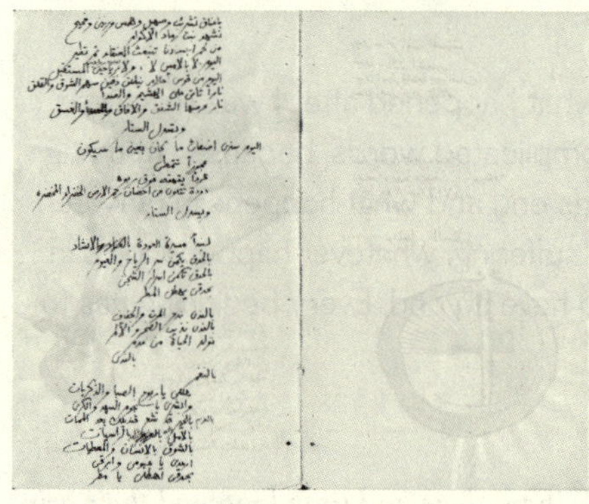

With craning necks, neighing, whisper-
ing, buzzing, and hissing,
We watch, as the piles of bodies come to
life from ashes.
From our flesh the phoenix rises and flies
away.
Today? No. Yesterday? No. Not even the
promising future's basil.
Today, from the bow of my dreams the
long-held arrow of longing and anxi-
ety sets off,
A fire that guts all debris and decay.
A fire as wide as the twilight, the hori-
zons, the dusk.
And the curtains are dropped.
Today we will see the chimeras of things
past with the eyes of what's to
become.

An old woman stretching her body,
A monkey guffawing on a hilltop,
A worm twirling in the embrace of the
green land's womb.
And the curtains were dropped.
Let's begin the homecoming parade with
chants.
In the eyes dwells the secret of the winds
and clouds.
In the eyes, the secrets of love are
secreted.
In my eyes falls the rain.
With dew, we can defeat death and
drought.
With dew, we can dissolve rocks and
pain.
Life is begotten from nothing.
By dew,
By melody.
Cheer up, Oh realms of youth and
memories.
Rejoice, Oh stars of sleeplessness and
slumber.
Your dead lantern is coming to life again.
Rejoice at the hopes, the solid resolve
At the outpouring longing, at man and
his potentials.
Thunder, Oh my clouds, and spark
lightning
On my eyes, do pour down. Oh rain.

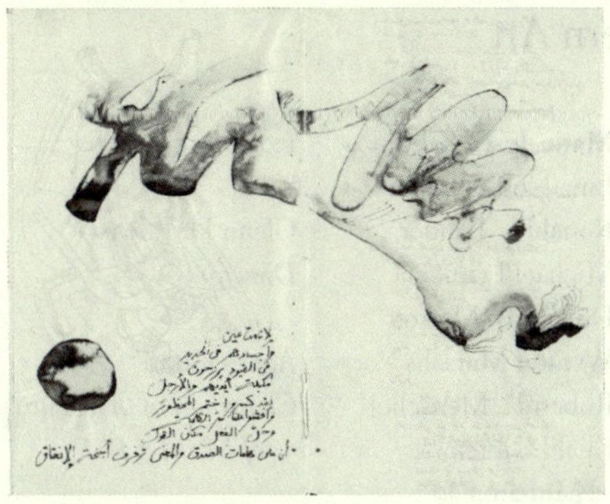

Sleepless eyes,
Their bodies, in iron shackles,
languishing,
Their hands and feet in chains.
They shattered the seal of prohibition,
And divulged, in public, the secret of the
word.
Deeds have replaced words.
On the foreheads of truthfulness, the
wings of emancipation flutter and flap.

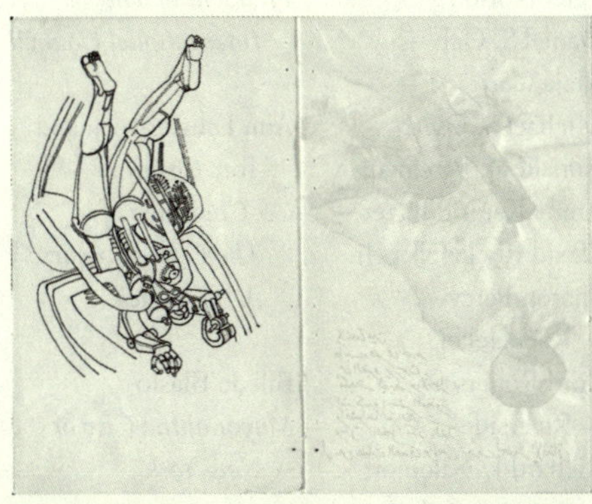

When things are upside down, they are apt to crash, because it doesn't make sense for things to be upside down. This figure has to be upright, on two feet. Here, the whole machinery of the state is facing downward, not upward.

This was an experience I went through for six months and eight days. But honestly it felt more like six years. Writing things frees you from the agony you have gone through and makes you feel like you no longer want to take revenge or take action. Basically, I know that I am not a politician, I am not an activist. I am someone who cares a great deal about human beings, a great deal about culture, a great deal about what human beings anywhere can communicate with others and the ideas and experiences they can exchange. And if that can help one person, it might be of some use.

Trustees of The Museum of Modern Art

Ronald S. Lauder
Honorary Chairman

Robert B. Menschel*
Chairman Emeritus

Agnes Gund*
President Emerita

Donald B. Marron
President Emeritus

Jerry I. Speyer
Chairman

Leon D. Black
Co-Chairman

Marie-Josée Kravis
President

Mimi Haas
Marlene Hess
Maja Oeri
Richard E. Salomon
Vice Chairmen

Glenn D. Lowry
Director

Richard E. Salomon
Treasurer

James Gara
Assistant Treasurer

Patty Lipshutz
Secretary

Wallis Annenberg*
Lin Arison**
Sarah Arison
Sid R. Bass*
Lawrence B. Benenson
Leon D. Black
David Booth
Eli Broad*
Clarissa Alcock Bronfman
Patricia Phelps de Cisneros
Steven Cohen
Edith Cooper
Douglas S. Cramer*
Paula Crown
Lewis B. Cullman**
David Dechman
Anne Dias Griffin
Glenn Dubin
Joel S. Ehrenkranz*
John Elkann
Laurence D. Fink
H.R.H. Duke Franz of Bavaria**
Glenn Fuhrman
Kathleen Fuld
Gianluigi Gabetti*
Howard Gardner
Maurice R. Greenberg**
Agnes Gund*
Mimi Haas
Marlene Hess
Ronnie Heyman
AC Hudgins
Barbara Jakobson*
Werner H. Kramarsky*
Jill Kraus

Marie-Josée Kravis
June Noble Larkin*
Ronald S. Lauder
Michael Lynne
Donald B. Marron*
Wynton Marsalis**
Robert B. Menschel*
Khalil Gibran Muhammad
Philip S. Niarchos
James G. Niven
Peter Norton
Daniel S. Och
Maja Oeri
Michael S. Ovitz
Ronald O. Perelman
Emily Rauh Pulitzer*
David Rockefeller, Jr.
Sharon Percy Rockefeller
Lord Rogers of Riverside**
Richard E. Salomon
Marcus Samuelsson
Ted Sann**
Anna Marie Shapiro*
Anna Deavere Smith
Jerry I. Speyer
Ricardo Steinbruch
Jon Stryker
Daniel Sundheim
Tony Tamer
Steve Tananbaum
Yoshio Taniguchi**
Jeanne C. Thayer*
Alice M. Tisch
Edgar Wachenheim III*
Gary Winnick

EX OFFICIO

Glenn D. Lowry
Director

Agnes Gund*
Chairman of the Board of MoMA PS1

Sharon Percy Rockefeller
President of The International Council

Ann Fensterstock and Tom Osborne
Co-Chairmen of The Contemporary Arts Council

Bill de Blasio
Mayor of the City of New York

Corey Johnson
Speaker of the Council of the City of New York

Scott M. Stringer
Comptroller of the City of New York

*Life Trustee
**Honorary Trustee

Sharjah Art Foundation

Sharjah Art Foundation is a legally independent public body established by Emiri Decree and supported by government funding, grants from national and international nonprofits and cultural organizations, corporate sponsors, and individual patrons.

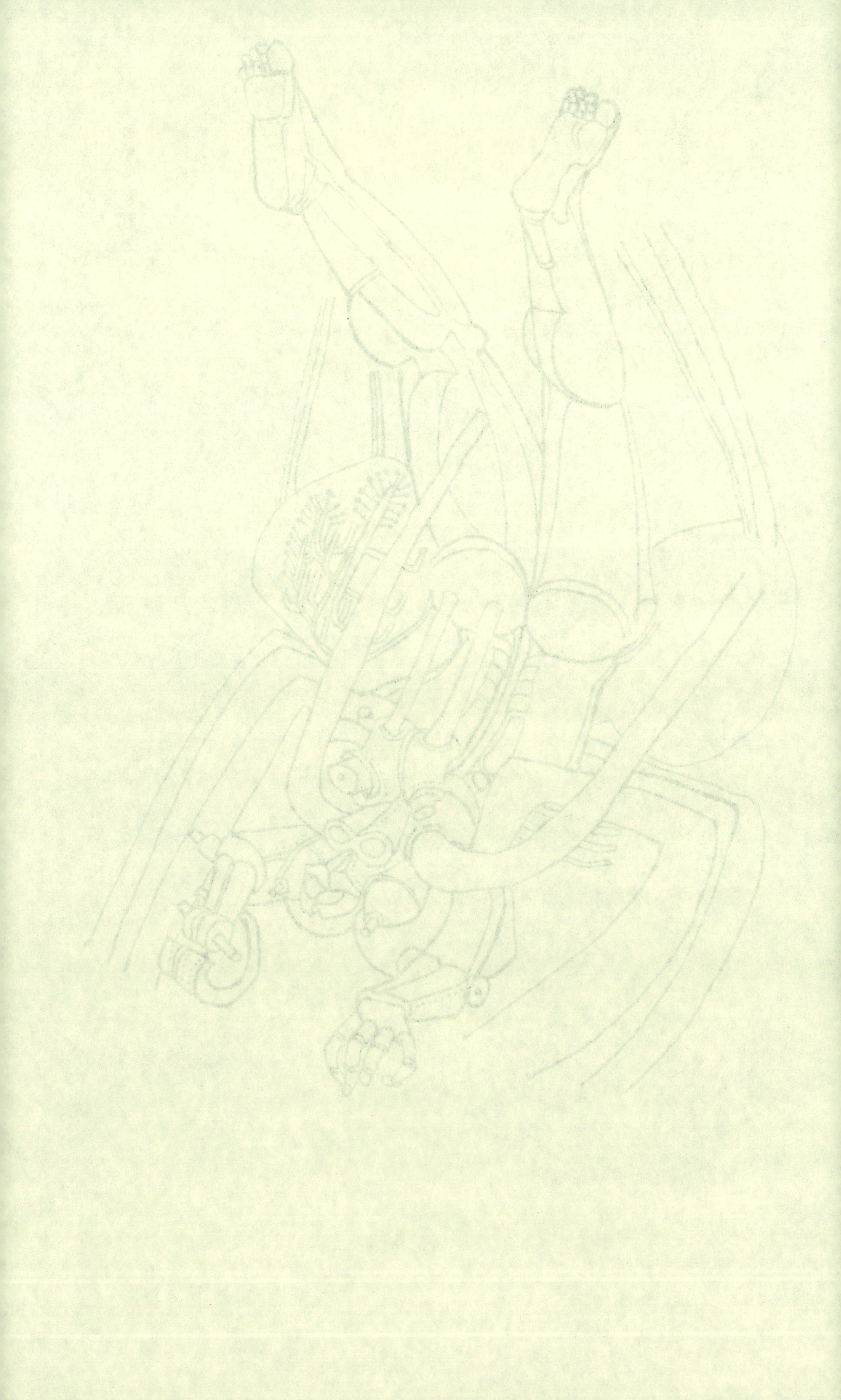

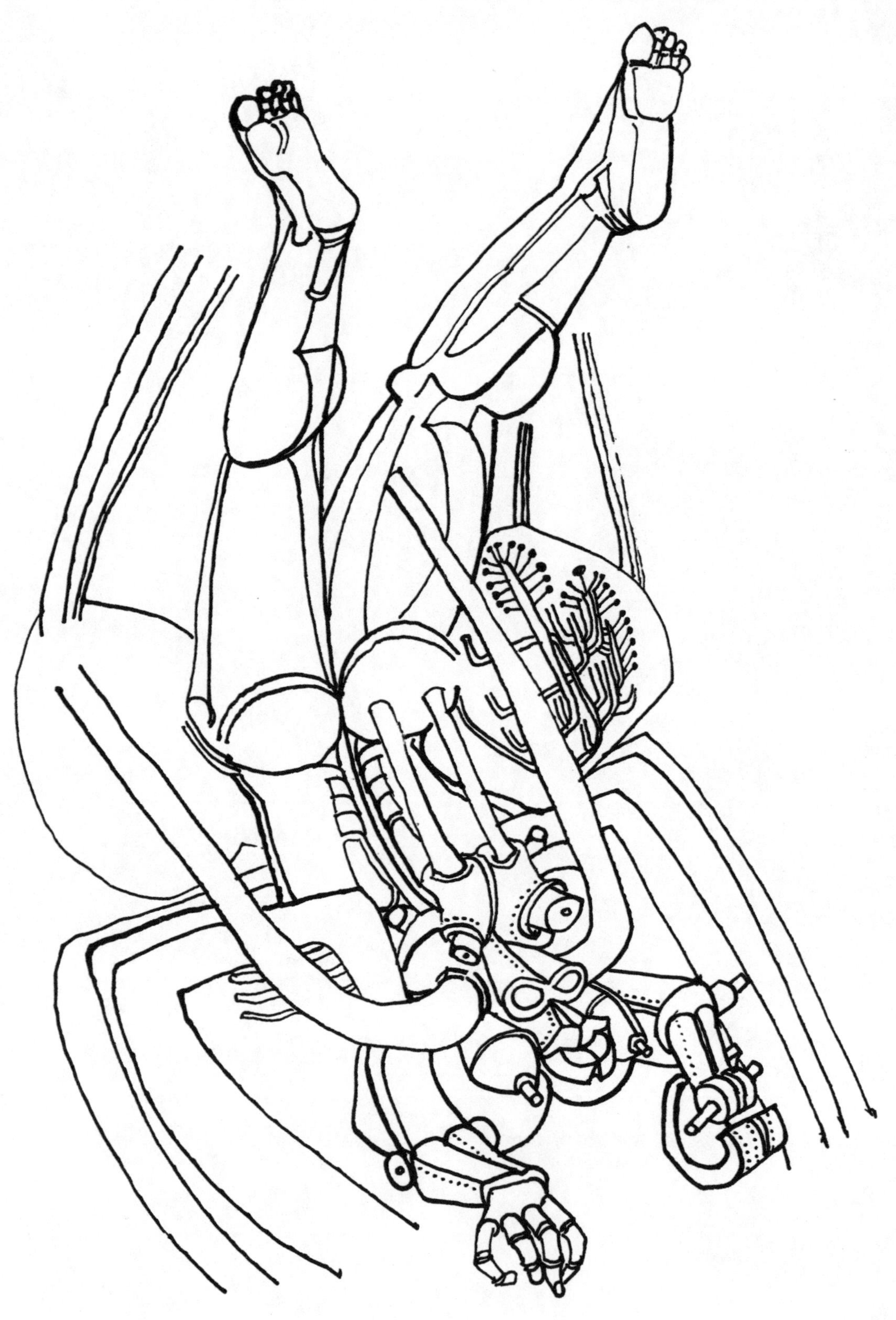

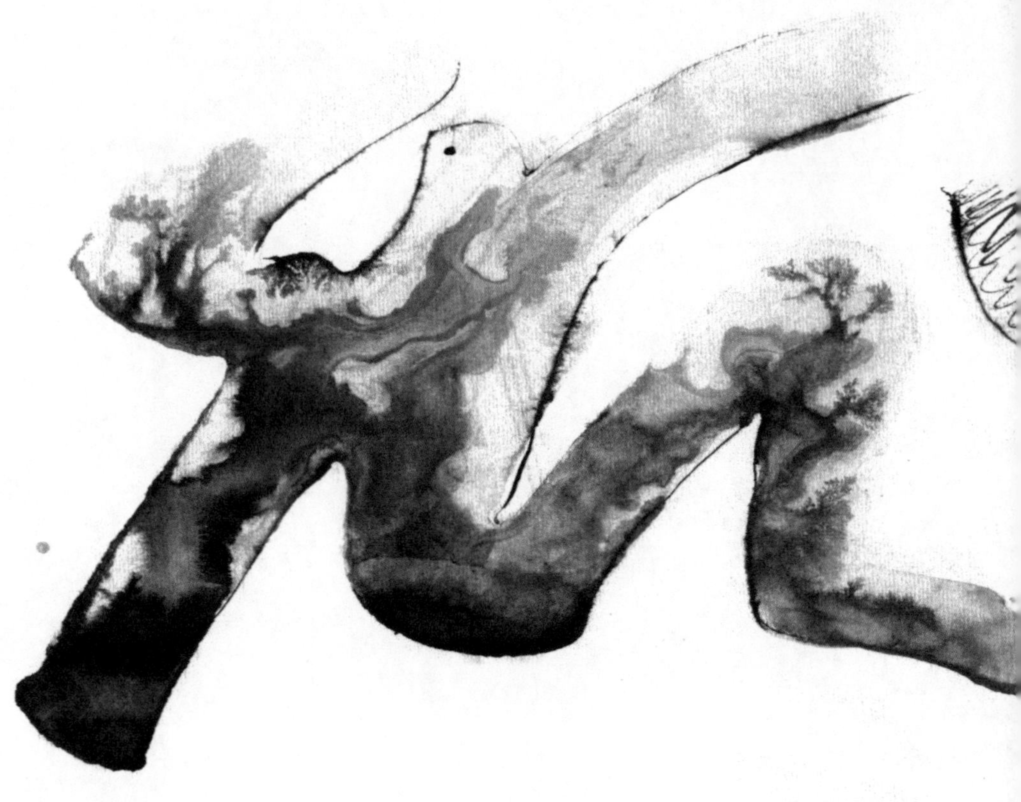

لا نامت عين
وأجسادهم في الحديد
في القيود يرزحون
مكبلة أيديهم والأرجل
لقد كسروا ختم المحظور
وأفشوا علينا سرّ الكلمة
وحلّ الفعل مكان القول
أن على هامات الصدق والمعنى ترفرف أجنحة الإنعتاق

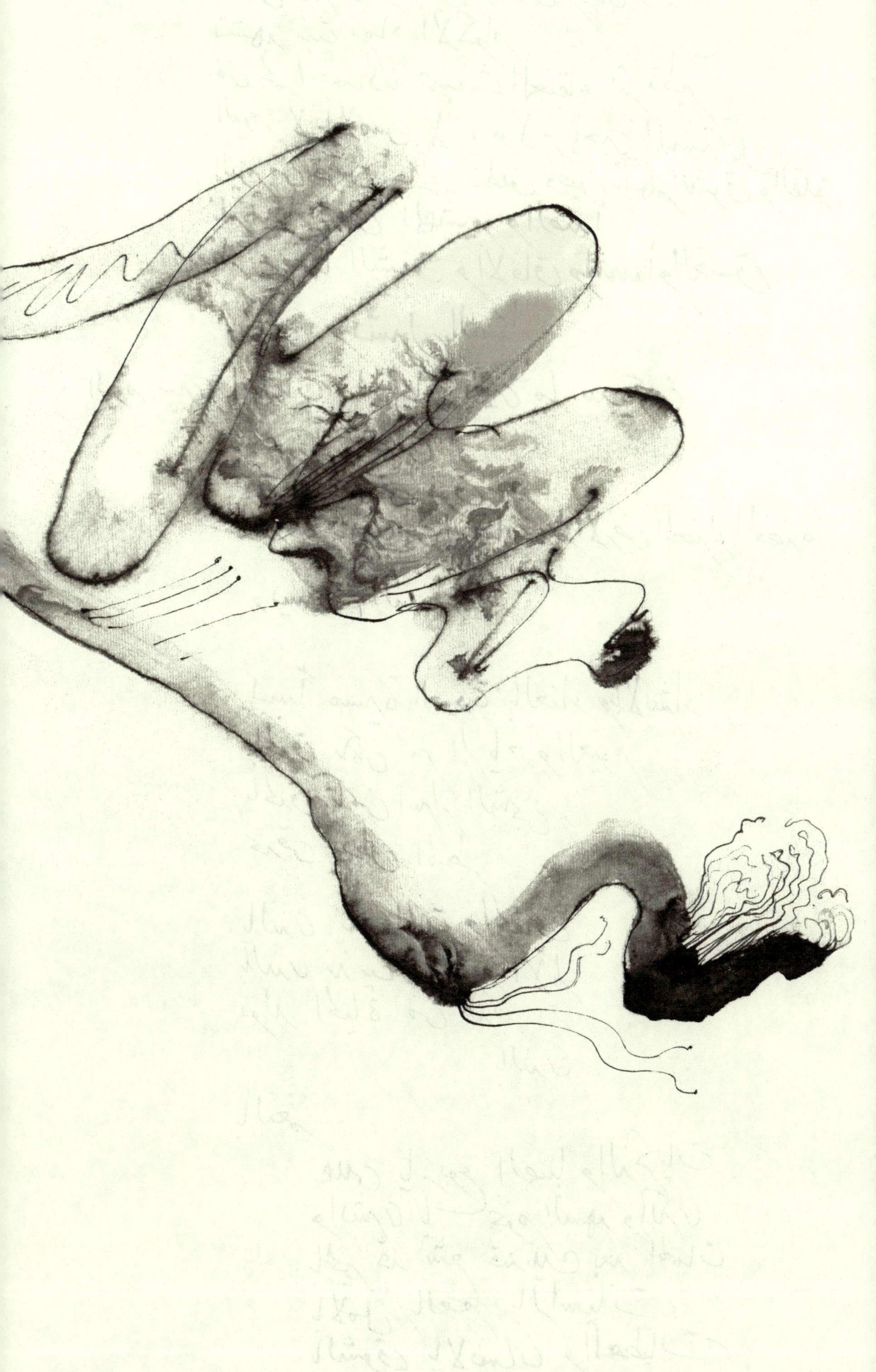

باعناق تشرئب وصهيل وهمس ورنين وضجيج
نشهد نبت رماد الإكرام
من لحم اجسادنا تنبعث العنقاء ثم تطير
اليوم - لا بالامس لا ، ولا برياحين المستقبل
اليوم من قوس أحلامي ينطلق دفين سهم الشوق والقلق
ناراً تأتي على الهشيم والصدا
نار عرضها الشفق والآفاق والغسق

ويسدل الستار

اليوم سنرى اضغاث ما كان بغير ما سيكون
عجوزاً تتمطى
قرداً يقهقه فوق ربوة
دودة تتلوى في احضان رحم الارض الخضراء المخضره

ويسدل الستار

لنبدأ مسيرة العودة بالغناء والانشاد
بالحدق يكمن سر الرياح والغيوم
بالحدق تكمن اسرار الشجن
بحدقي يهطل المطر

بالندى نذبح الموت والجفاف
بالندى نذيب الصخر والألم
تولد الحياة من عدم
بالندى

بالنغم
هلّلي يا ربوع الصبا والذكريات
والتثري يا نجوم السهد والكرى
بالخير قد شع قنديلك بعد الممات
بالأمل بالعزم بالراسيات
بالشوق بالانسان والمعطيات
ارعدي يا غيوم وابرقي
بحدقي اهطلي يا مطر

بيدي سافتح استار المستقبل
بيدي سأكتب اشعاري
بيدي اسطر مكتوب يوم الممات
بيدي اصور رسم الكلام
بيدي

الرمز حرف يجري ويتعرّج
يصعد ويهبط ويصغر ويتدحرج
ويخط دوائر حول الأكوام
وتجف الأقلام

وتسدل الستار

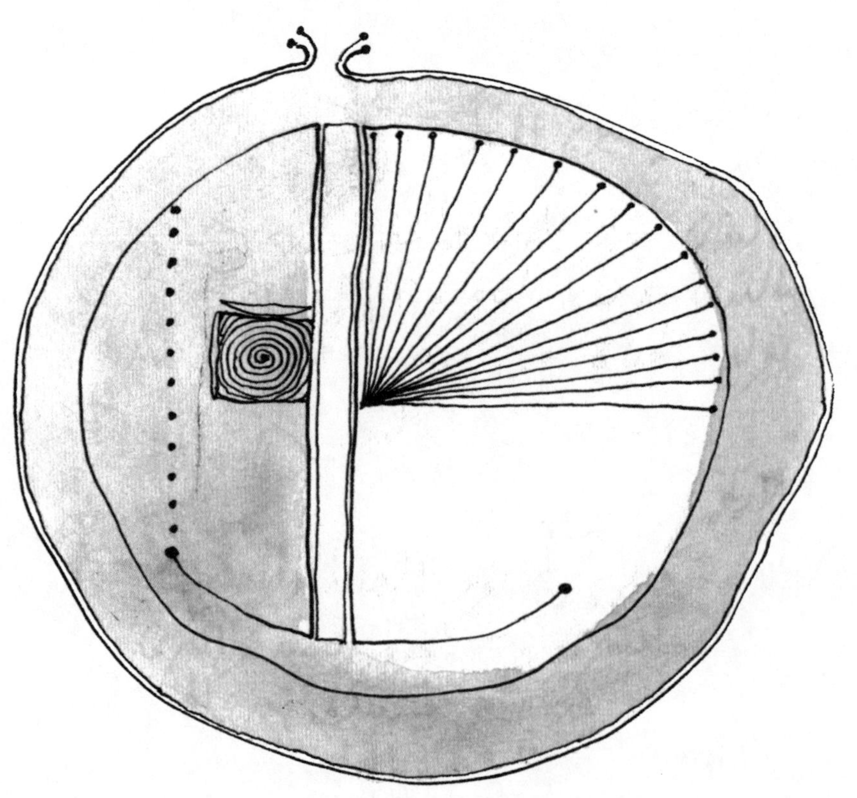

يوم احتجب الضوء
وران كم لازج الصمت على كل فكر ونغم
~~يوم عم الصدأ~~

يوم نما الصخر حتى شارف ~~نبتة~~ البنح عنان السماء
وانسد باب المنفذ والمخرج
~~وعم الركود والصدأ~~

يومها كانت البداية

يوم ~~ألقت~~ تفجرت الارض ~~أثقالها~~ والقت احمالها وأثقالها
~~وبذت احمالها ومآلها~~
وارخت قبضة المكان والزمان إسارها وأسوارها
وانطلق سهم القلق صوب الجبين
~~واصاب هامة وراء حجب خلف الجبين~~ يصيب
يومها انشق الستر والسربال
~~انصدع~~ قناع وجهنا القديم تصدع
وانشق سقف السرداب
فانكشفت تجاعيد الغور وبانت اخاديد الشوق الدفين
لافظة احداثه نحوش النائمين

ليتبدل الاستار

ولينطق الاخرس المخرس

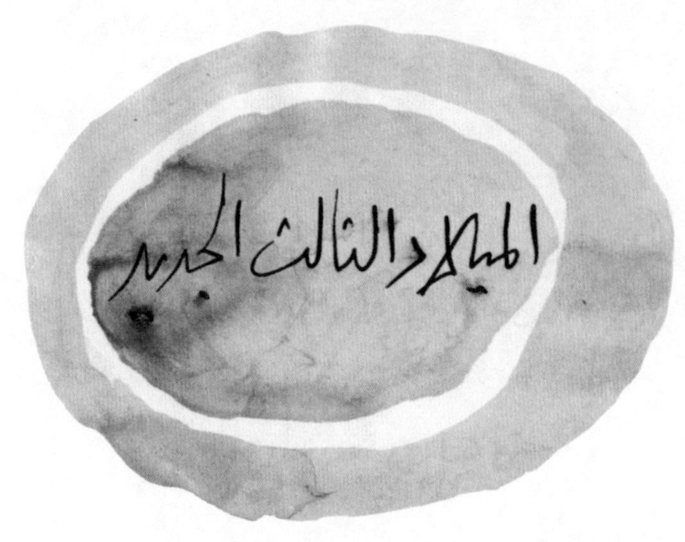

وتسدل الستار
هكذا كما يقولون قد بدأت المأساة
وهكذا تنزوي وهكذا
وهكذا نقول ونقول هكذا ونقول ونقول وهكذا

....

بغلائل دخان الماضي يلتحف الكون والسكون
بلسان الصمت المحرق أقرع باب الابواب
لينطق الاخرس لينطق الاخرس لينطق الاخرس
وتسدل الستار
ثم ياتي يوم البدء
يوم انحنى عود الزمان
واحدودب ظهر الارض
وذبلت نضارة السهول والوهاد
ونضب الكأس
فغاض مجرى النهر تحت أنهار السراب
وغشيت سحب التراب كل حدق
يوم عاد التراب الى التراب كانت البداية

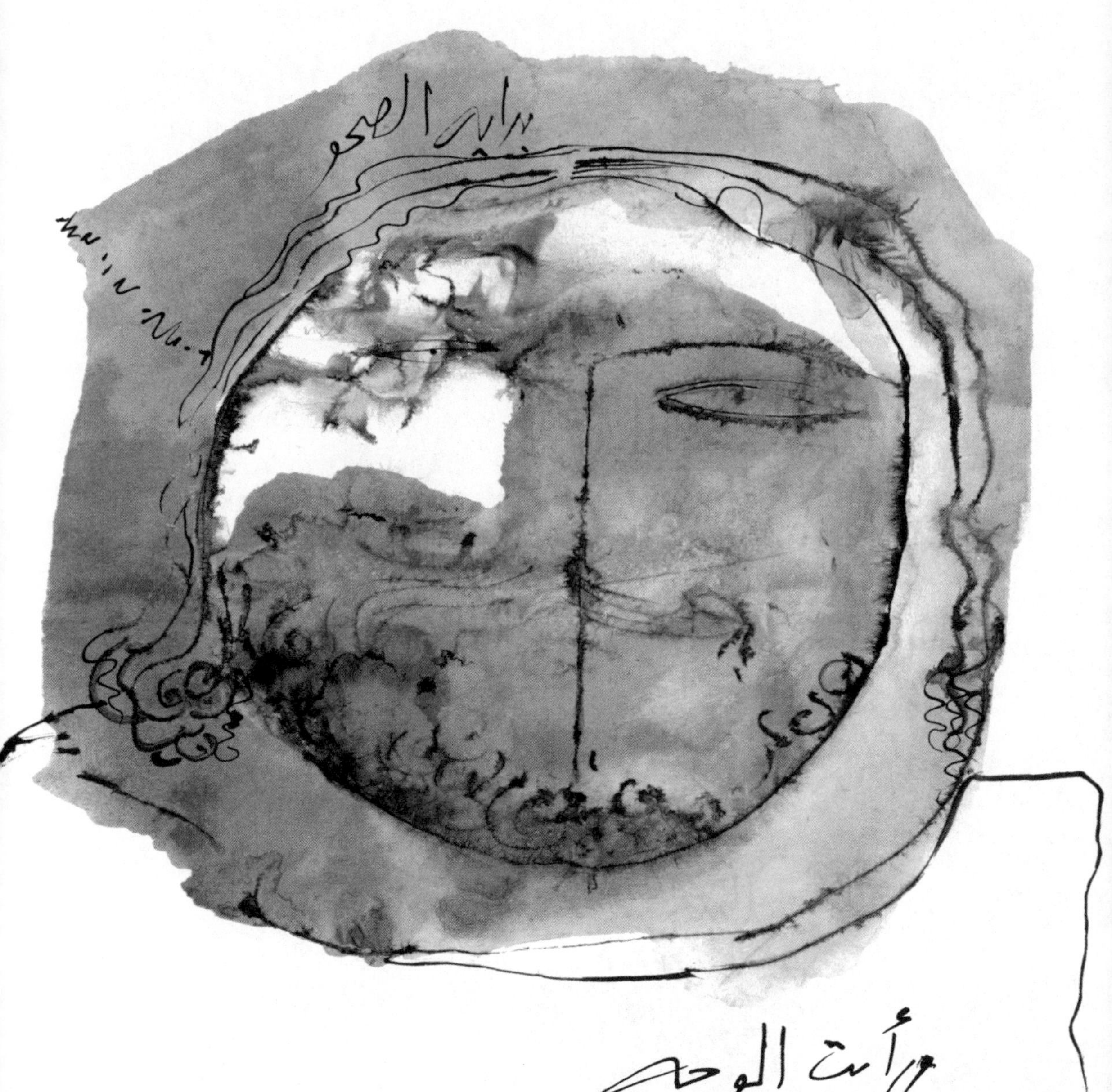

رأيت الوجه
وجه الأمل الحنون
صبوح في تناسقه عجيب
نوراني مشع بالضياء جبين
رأسه في حجر زوجه تنثر الماء عليه
يغالب الآلام والسكرات والأنين
رآني وابتسم
فنسيت الموت والنسيان والسجون

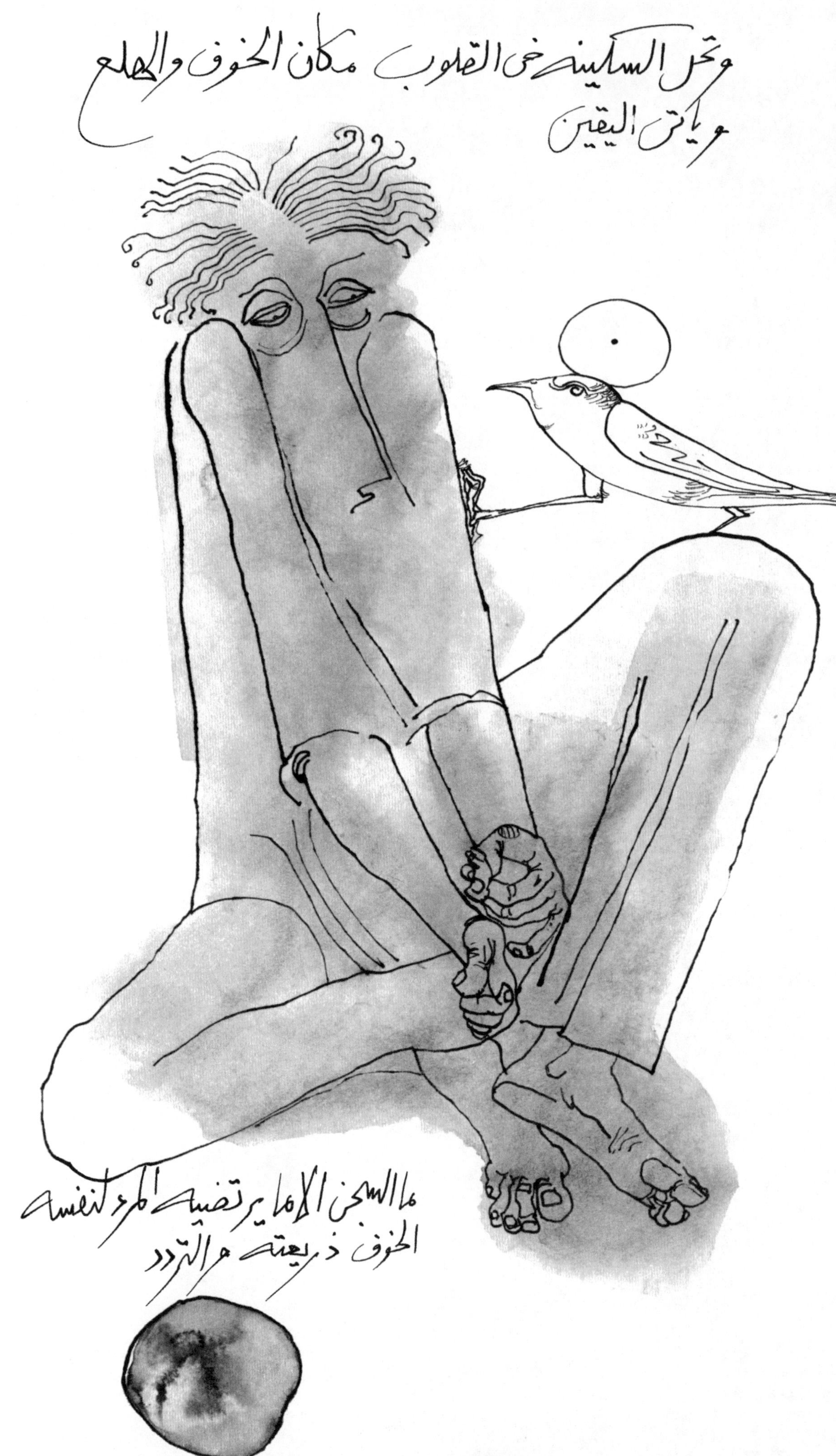
وتحل السكينة في القلوب مكان الخوف والهلع
ويأتي اليقين
ما السجن إلا ما يرتضيه المرء لنفسه
الخوف ذريعته مع التردد

الإبتلاء

بالضيق بالهم بالنكد
بالقهر بالعسر بالحرمان
كلها في مسيرة الإنسان شواهد تستبين معها صلابة
المعدن والإيمان.

والوعد الحق

إنّ بعد العسر يسرا
إنّ بعد العسر يسرا

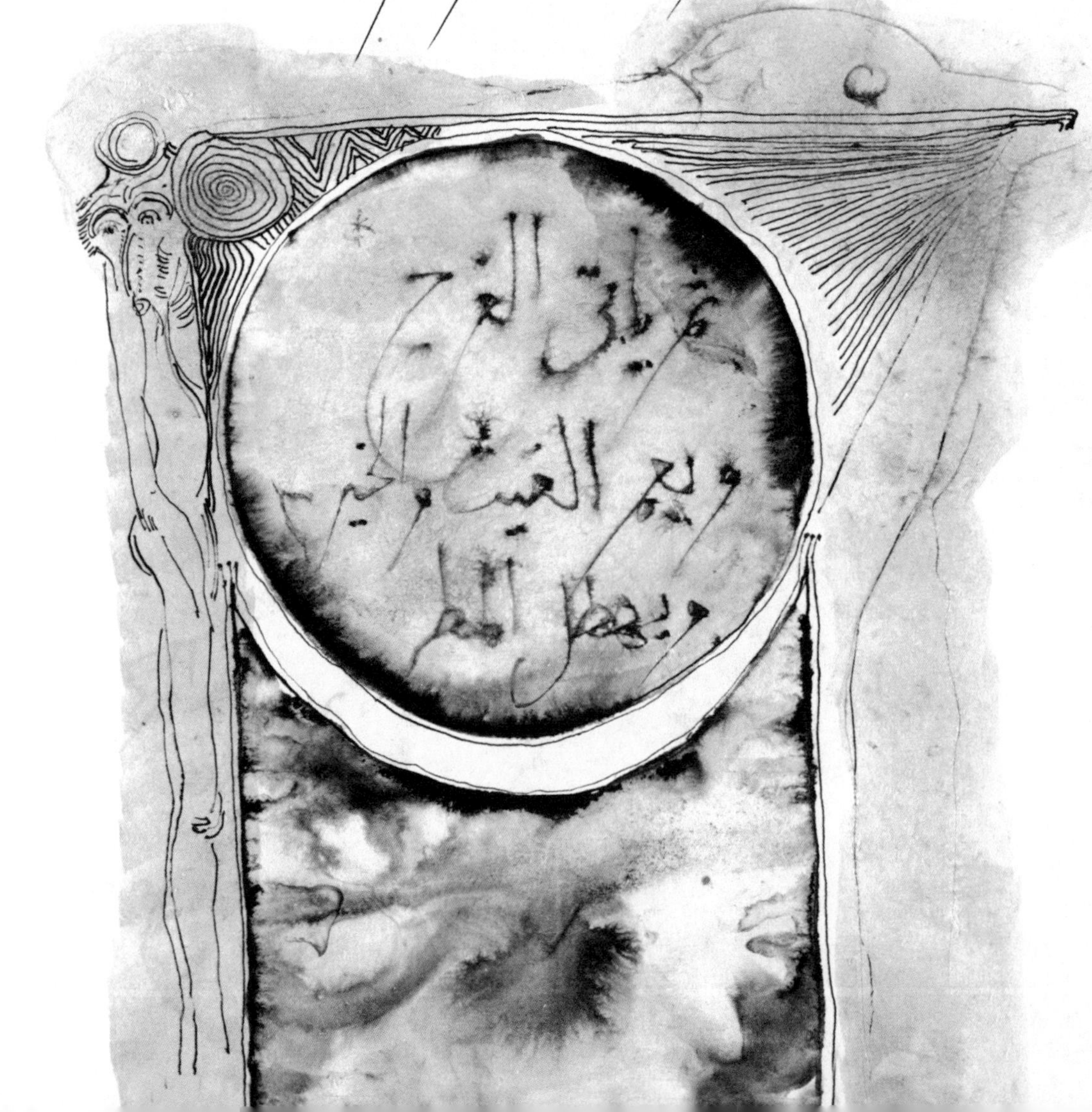

ثم يأتي الفرج
ويعم الغيث والخير
ويهطل المطر

انفاق بعرض الجسد ملتوية ودروب قدت من كتل بركانية
ازحف فيها ثعباناً واجوس بلا نور هادٍ
واسمع أقدام الحرّاس يسدون الباب المنفذ وأتوه بلا نور هادٍ بلا ابواب بلا مخرج
واحاول ارجع ادراجي ويسد الحراس المنفذ
واجوس بلا نورٍ هادٍ انفاقاً ودروباً ملتوية ، وأتوه ، أتوه ، صراخي لا يسمع وفمي مطبق .
صراخي لن يسمع وفمي مطبق

وجدت أن قد تم نقلنا الى زنازين أخر
غرب الزنازين الحاليه
تجري من الجنوب صوب الشمال حال المحابس الشرقيه
لونها كالح السواد كئيبه المنظر

أمامها ساحة طينيه
الطحالب والماء الآسن يكسوها طين آسن
وقيل لنا اخرجوا
فخرجت على هيئة ثعبان أحلك
عبر أبواب ثلاث
دفعة واحدة وحدي
ولم يخرج غيري

وتمددت على الأرض ساكنا دون حراك
رأسي عند الجنوب ارقب الشمس عند المشرق
وجيء بسكين كالمنشار
كشراع مراكب النيل الخشبيه
مجتثا رأسي عند العنق
وبترت الذيل
وعندها جف رأسي وعنقي وذيلي
وقطعت باقي جسدي الى ثلاثه اقسام متساويه

واختفى السكين
وتلاشى رأسي عنقي ذيلي، ذيل الثعبان
وبقي باقي جسدي
ظهري كالتمساح ثلاث كتل مشويه
واختفى الثعبان
فجريت أبحث عن رأسي وذيلي وعنقي المبتوره

وقيل لنا ارجعوا الى جحوركم
فرجعت دون ان ادور
دفعة واحدة خلفي عبر الابواب
ثلاثه أحجار بلوريه

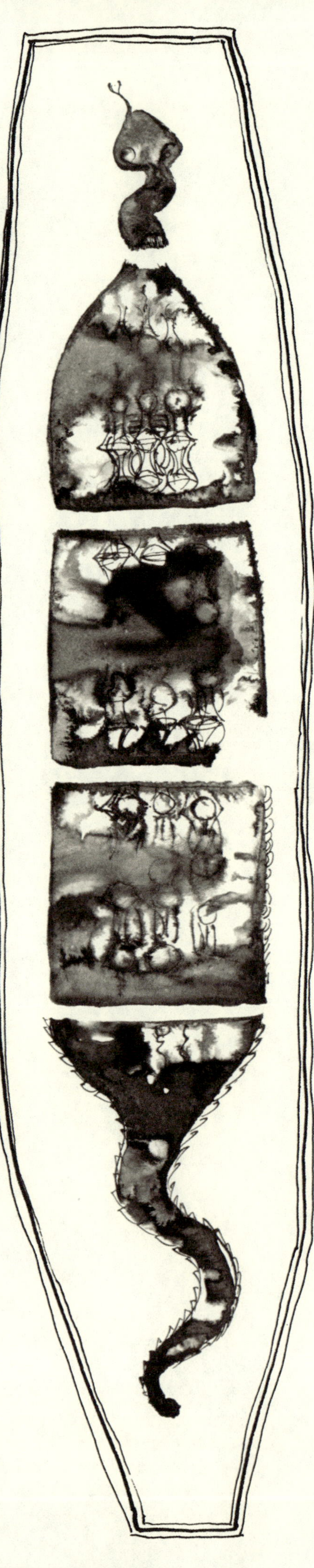

وسرى ذكرها العذب مسرى النسيم على وجه الرمضاء الأغبر

أتى العسكر، كسروا باب الزنزانة
بالمدفع من خط أفقي شقوا صدري
وتناثر دماً من كل إتجاه ومدى
جرّوا جسدي خارج أبواب بركانية
كفني أبيض أحمر أبيض أحمر أبيض

أخذوا جسدي نحو الغرب نحو مراقد الغرباء
وواروني تراب الغرباء عند المغرب

وفار دمي وأنا أنظر في لحدي دون ألم

وكال العسكر مزيداً من تراب
وتصدوا بالمدفع والرشاش

ودمي غالب
فوق النهر، عند المعبر، يخترق دمي صف العسكر
سار واندفع نحو المدفع، صوب القصر، عبر المدفع
وصعد، من القدم الحافي وعلا فوق القامة
تحت دمي غرق الطاغوت
وأنا أنظر في لحدي دون ألم

ارتفع الى عنان السماء حائط من تراب أصفر
تبعه الاحمر ثم الاخضر ثم حائط أسود
وانكشف الحائط عنه
دهمة تتشكل، يختال على صورة انسان يمشي
يخب في مشية من يمشي ويستوي على اربعة
الحرير والديباج له وبر
لعابه الشهد يسيل
نابه العاج والرخام والمرمر
ريحه المسك والريحان والعنبر
على جبينه رسم عنقود الملذات الرطيب
قنديل مفتاح الحياة الدنيوية

ثم كانت هيئته يوم أتى
صارخا بين السهول والوهاد بأعلى همهمة
يصيح منحدرا من أعالي الجبال نحو الأزرق
كلكم اتباعي كلكم اتباعي ومريدي
من له منكم صمم أشتريه
من له صوت نخاف احبسه
بشريتكم رسول الاصلاح انا منقذ البشرية جمعاء
الخلاص انا
ويبح صوته فتسمع صلصلة الخرائب بين فكيه

يمد يدا الى حلقومه ينتزع صوتا أخطبوطي الجذور سفلي الأثر
يضع الصوت عن شماله وباليمين يأتي بالمحرقة وبالسندان وبالمطرقة
لمطرقة، يغمسه في زيت القنديل، يعيده الى الحنجرة
وينادي في سحر البلبل المغرد
من يضمن لي الخلود أضمن له السعادة الأبدية
وجاء بالعراف وبالقداح السبع الاسطورية
سهمه طائش في الفضاء فتتكسر لصداه خيوط الضوء المنثورة
وتغمض الشمس جفنيها ويسود الظلام الابدي
وينبلج من جهة الشرق نجم أزرق
وتسمع في الكون جلجلة الصاعقة
فتنقسم بذرة الخير والشر، وتنفصم الأسطورة
فدبج
وجيء عندها بالموت
هو زال حائط الوهم ومات الدجال
بموت الدجل

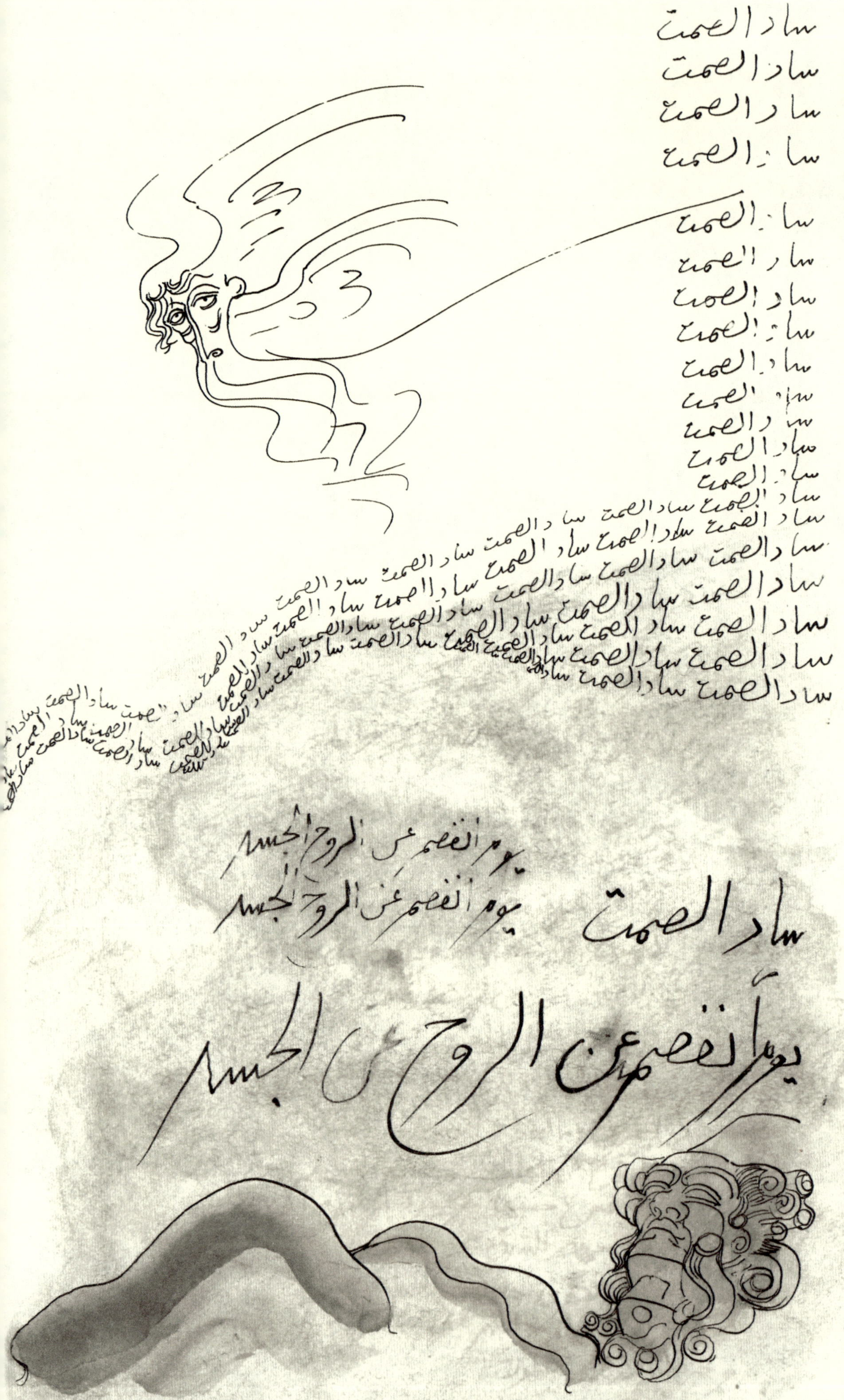

ساد الصمت
ساد الصمت
ساد الصمت
ساد الصمت

ساد الصمت
ساد الصمت
ساد الصمت
ساد الصمت
ساد الصمت
ساد الصمت
ساد الصمت
ساد الصمت
ساد الصمت
ساد الصمت ساد الصمت ساد الصمت
ساد الصمت ساد الصمت ساد الصمت ساد الصمت
ساد الصمت ساد الصمت ساد الصمت ساد الصمت ساد الصمت
ساد الصمت ساد الصمت ساد الصمت ساد الصمت ساد الصمت ساد الصمت
ساد الصمت ساد الصمت ساد الصمت ساد الصمت ساد الصمت ساد الصمت
ساد الصمت ساد الصمت ساد الصمت ساد الصمت ساد الصمت ساد الصمت
ساد الصمت ساد الصمت ساد الصمت ساد الصمت ساد الصمت ساد الصمت
ساد الصمت ساد الصمت ساد الصمت ساد الصمت ساد الصمت
ساد الصمت ساد الصمت ساد الصمت ساد الصمت

يوم انفصم عن الروح الجسد
يوم انفصم عن الروح الجسد

ساد الصمت

يوم انفصم عن الروح الجسد

بيتي
ورقي قلمي خرشاتي

بنتي
ولدي زوجتي
أحبابي

الرقبة تطول
كالجمل كالديناصور
أفعى تسعى
حشرجة في عش العصفور

وصلّى الشهداء على أرواح الشهداء الطاهرة
وانهمر الدمع إذ يبس الحلقوم
وجفت الشفاه
وتشقق الكلام
يوم انكسر عود الكلمة
عند مفترق الزمان والمكان

مات يوم تقلّص وانزوى أفضل الجهاد عندنا
مات الإنسان
نحو أخيه الإنسان

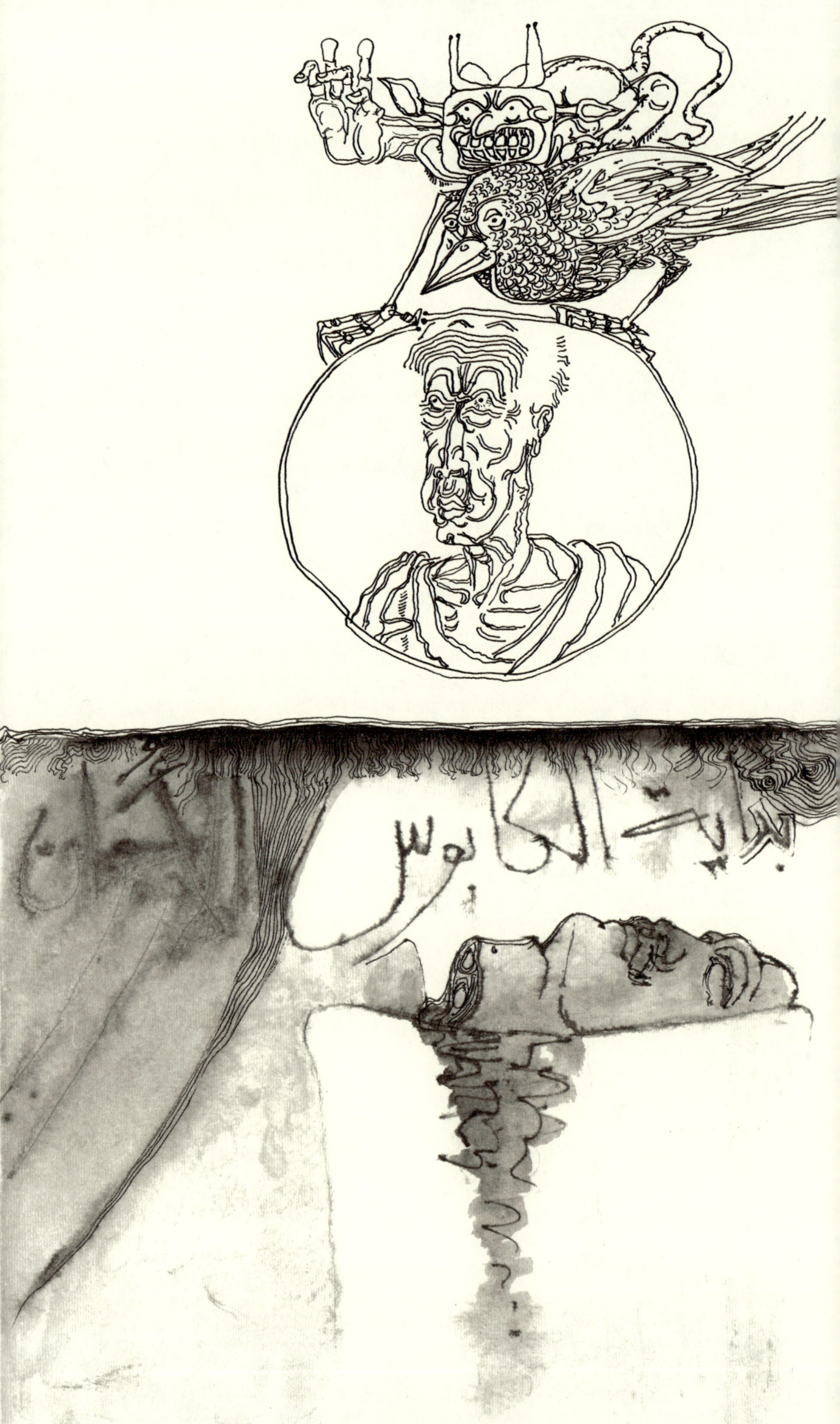

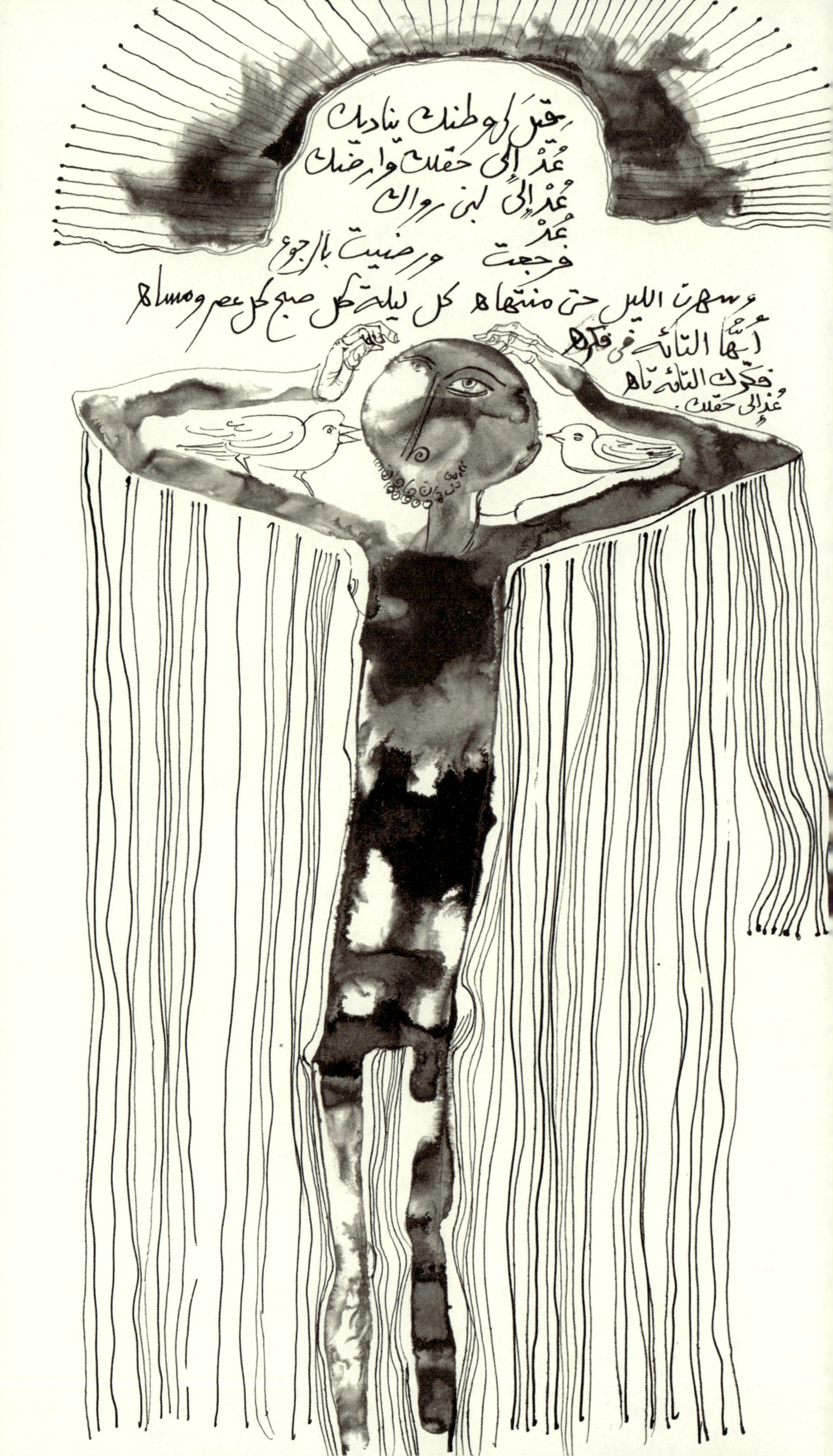
حقل كرم وطنك يناديك
عُدْ إلى حقلك وأرضك
عُدْ إلى لبن رواك
عُدْ
فرجعت ورضيت بالرجوع
وسهرت الليل حتى منتهاه كل ليلة كل صبح كل عصر ومساء
أيها التائه في فكره
فكرك التائه تاه
عُدْ إلى حقلك.

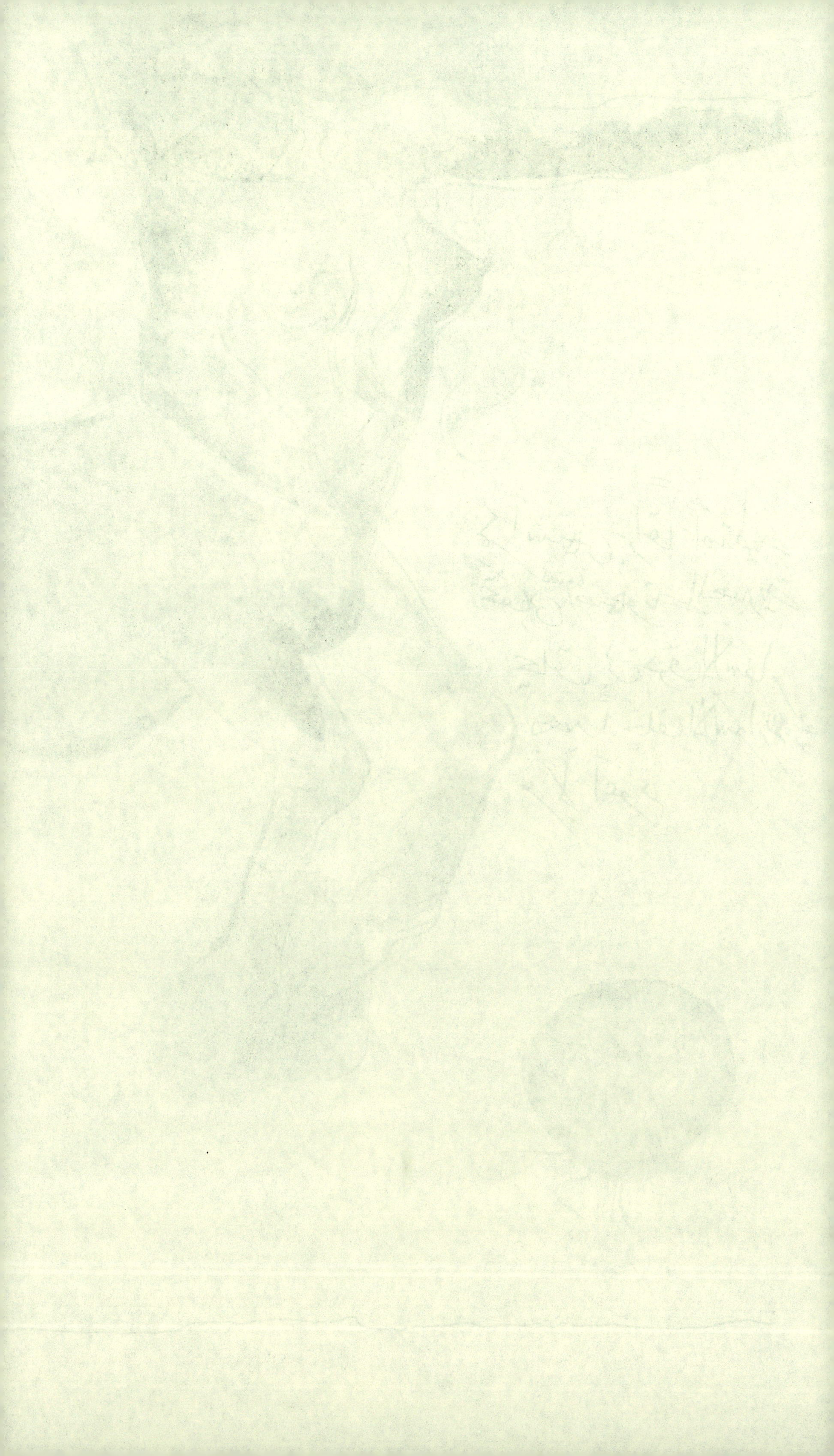

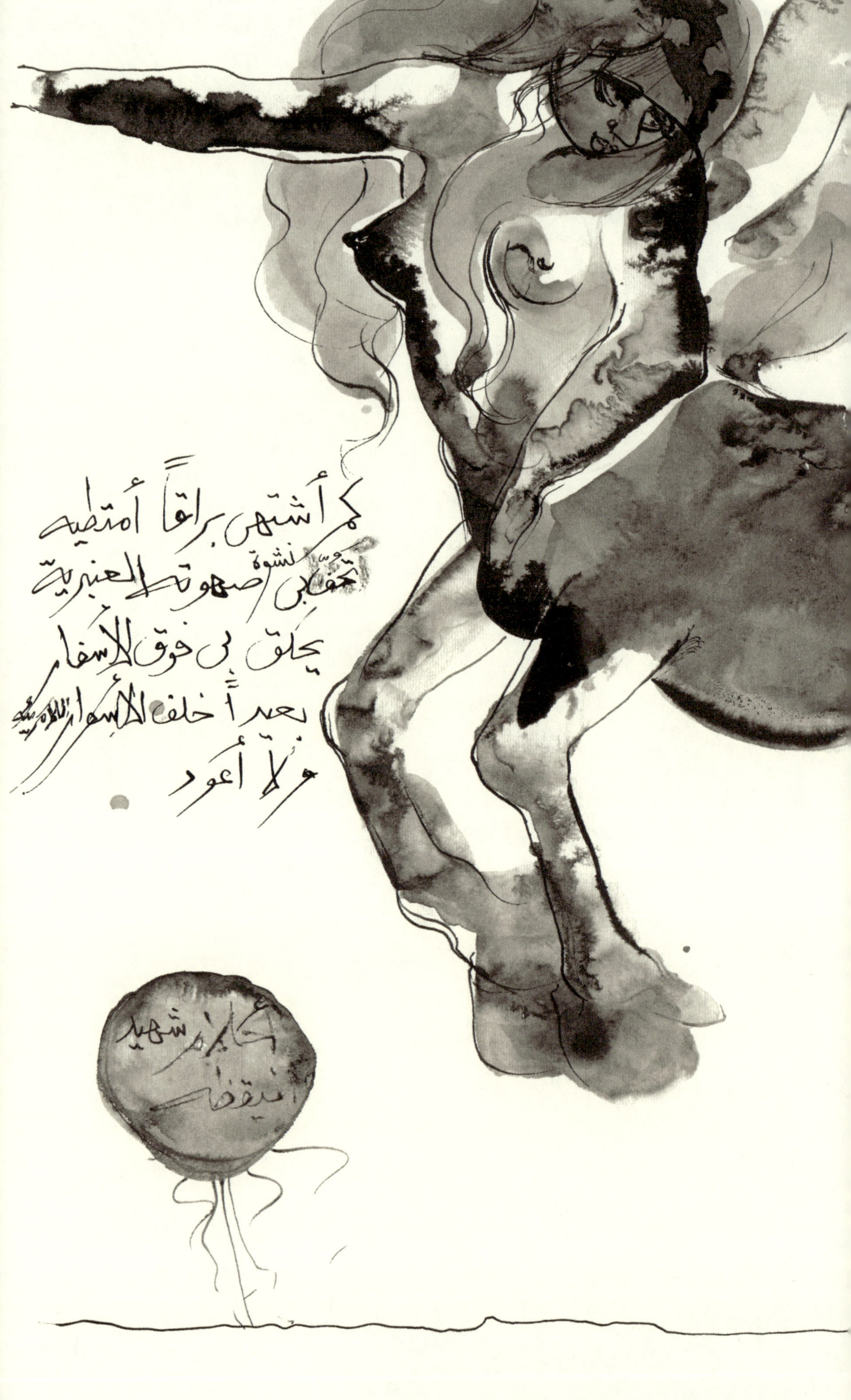
كم أشتهي براقاً أمتطيه
نشوة
تحفني صهوته العنبرية
يحلق بي فوق الأسفار
بعيداً خلف الأسوار
ولا أعود
أحلام شهيد

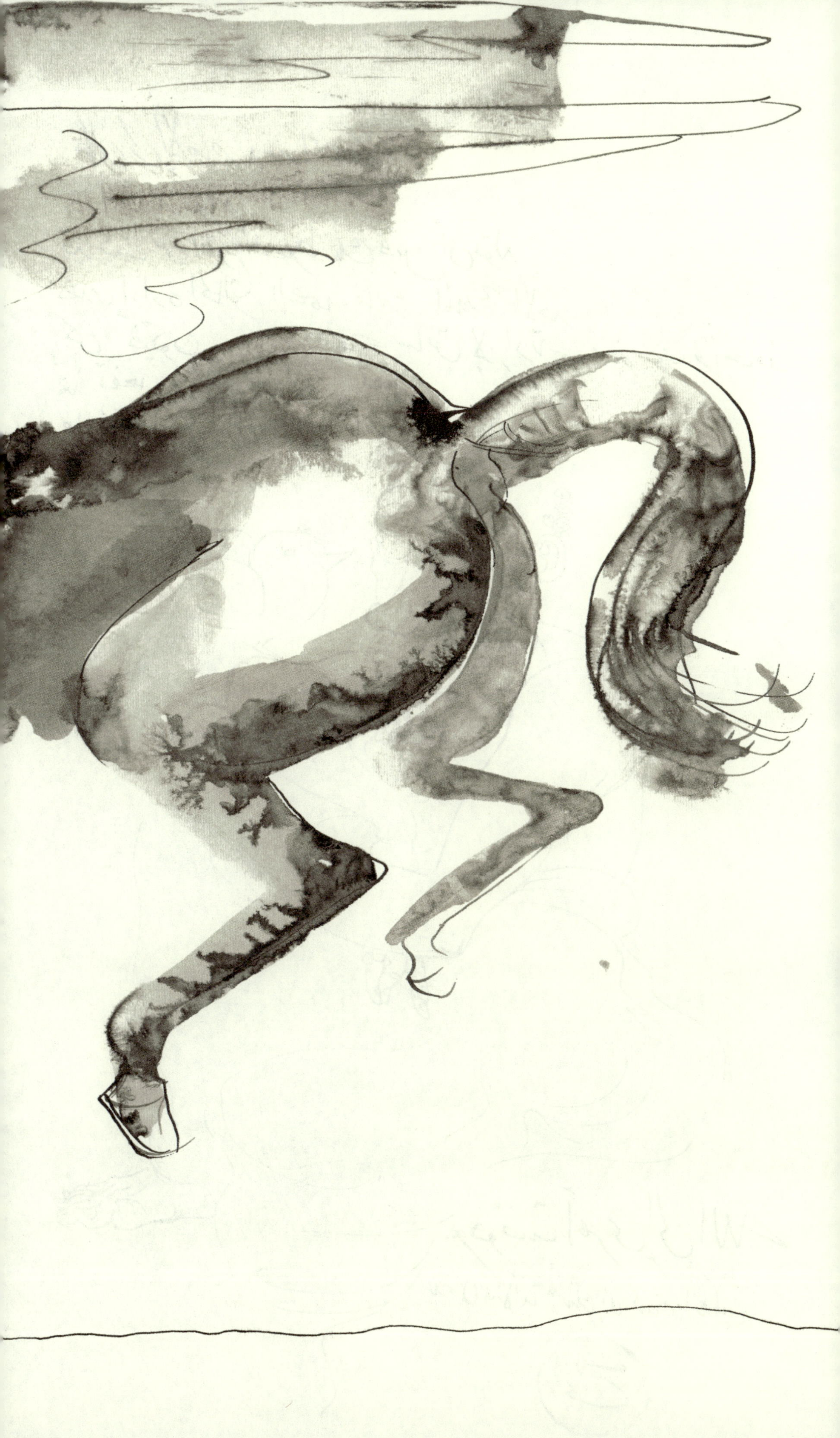

قال لي الإمام بعد الصلاة
هذا قضاء وقدر
قد كتب في اللوح المحفوظ لك قبل أن تولد
هذي إرادة الخالق الصمد، مالك الملك الأحد
كن فيكون ، علمه سابق لإرادته، قد سوى وأحاط
فما تفعل سوى أن تقبل
وما أفعل سوى أن أقبل

وفوضت أمري إلى الله

انه لا اله الا أنت سبحانك إني كنت من الظالمين

وأتى الحرّاس ضباطاً وعسكر
اليوم تنقلون
قالوها أوامراً لنا بلا سؤال بلا طلب
الكوارنتينة
كل معتقل عليه تحت أبطه حمل المتاع
لم تكن لي لا حصيرة لا غطاء
ما على بدني سوى قميص وسروال قد اتسخ
لم أذق طعم السواك ليلتي تلك ولا هذا الصباح
لا مشطاً تخلل لحيتي رأسي تخلله التراب
وداعاً أيها الأصحاب وداعاً أيها الأحباب
لله كالعهد توثيقاً ومعرفة وقرباً والتصاق
الآن والى الأبد
وسرنا كل في إتجاه
عبر أسوار وحيطان وأبواب حديد
قد رأيت الوجه وجه المعتقل
خلف كوة عتيقة لزنازين عتيقة
قيل: جرذها جوعى، تقضم الأطراف والأصابع
ودخلنا
الباب أغلق خلفنا كالرعد هولاً كالجبل
وبالمزلاج، سمكه الساق، سمكه الذراع والقدم
ولقيناهم سبقونا اليه واحد وأربعة
سلام على أهل الديار سلام على الأرض
سلام من الله أهل المعتقل
سلام من الله لأهل المعتقل

عددهم خمساً وخمسين ومنضدة عليها سلة ومقصلة
قالوا انها دُرّة أنها دُرّة إنها سر عظيم الشان
يداوي السمّ والأشجان
واحد منا كهم قائل، لا سلام على طعام، لا سلام
طعام السجن لا طعم له بلا ألوان
بلا ملح بلا كنه يبل الريق، بلا سائل
بلا لحم بلا عظم بلا أسنان

واحد منا كهم سائل:
ومن أنتم
وقالوا حزب تحرير، طريق الحق والاسلام
عضضنا عليه بالنواجذ
يقول جاسوساً معهم
انا حزبي قديم محترف
عامل حركي
همي أن أجمع شمل أهل الحق سراً شغلي الشاغل
يقول سائلنا كنا سراً
حذار
لا تقولوا أي شيء لا تقولوا أي كلام
عينه عين النظام
إنه عواصة يسمع لنا، انهم الغام
عينه عين النظام
الخوف والشك وسوء الظن دستور النظام
لا سقى الظل هوان
ونفضت الثوب والطاعوت عن بدني
نفضت الجهم والالام
نفضت عني الأحزان والآهات والأشجان
لا سقى ظل هوان، لا سقى ظل هوان

لا سقى الظلُ حرثاً نبته خوف وذل وهوان

فابريقة
السعادة
الطائرة

ونغني كما يغني الطير أحلى
ونطير فوق الربى والوادي
شعرها كالكدملة أزيز
نغم معدني لا يدانيه نغم
ويذاع من محطات الإذاعة
بكل يوم بكل طرف كل ساعة
يا محطات الإذاعة المعدنية
رحمة بالناس من هذي السعادة
رحمة بالناس من هذي السعادة

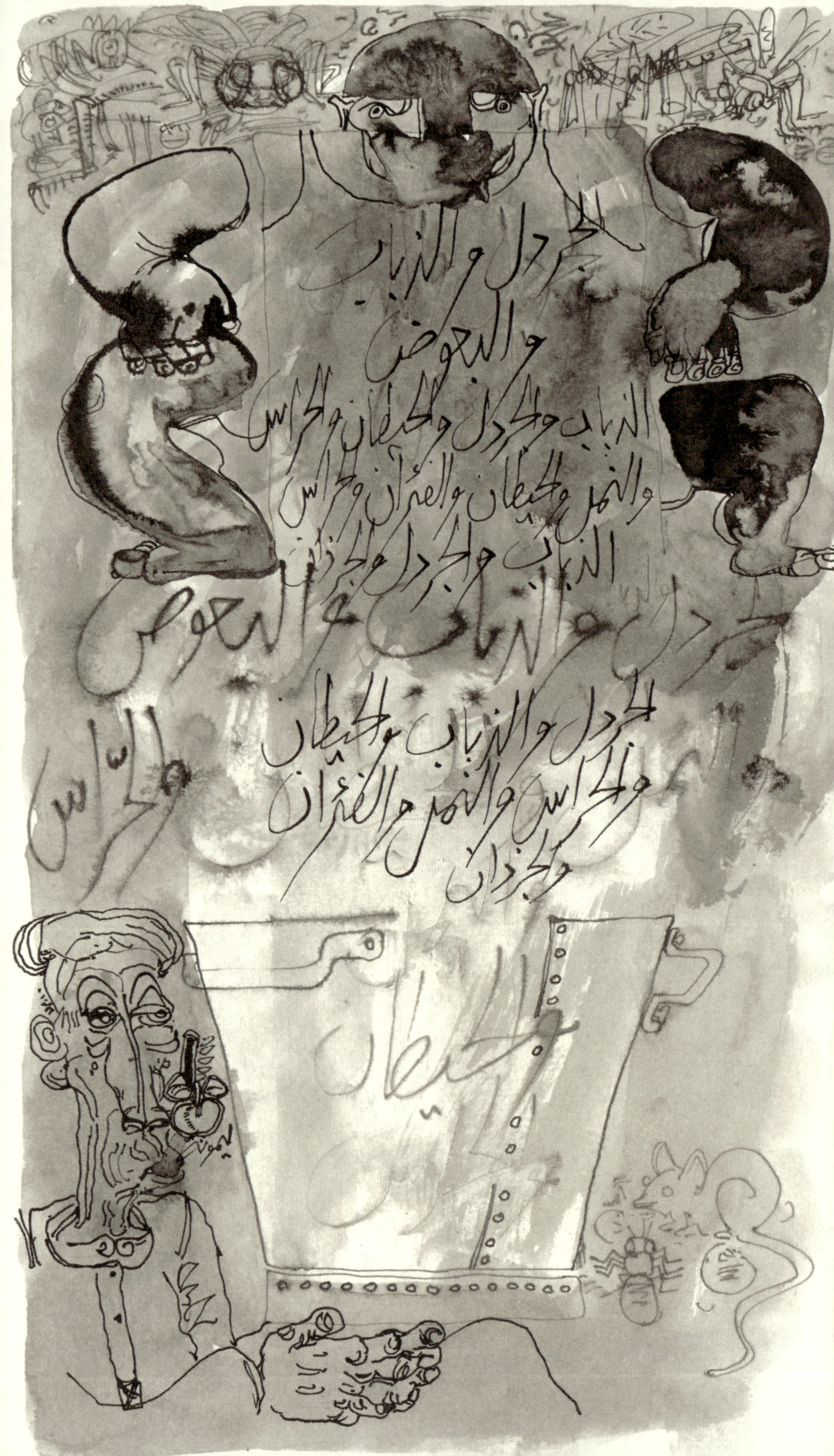
الجردل والذباب
والبعوض
الذباب والجردل والحيطان والحراس
والنمل والحيطان والفئران والحراس
الذباب والجردل والجرذان
الجردل والذباب والبعوض
الجردل والذباب والحيطان
والحراس والنمل والفئران
والجرذان
والحراس
والحيطان

اليوم لا نوم لا إستلقاء بعد التمام
كل الحصائر في ركن
المنتظرون يكنسون يمسحون ويكنسون
كل الملابس في ركن
ويمسحون
وينثرون الرمل فوق العيون
اليوم يوم المرور
يوم سبت أول اسبوع أول الشهر
جاءوا يهرولون ينظرون
وجاء على عجل
بسمة كالشهد
عوجة ما في
عوجة ما في سعادتك
كيف
وثار بركاني
عن الانسان عن الحقوق عن الدستور
عن القانون عن الانسان الانسان
والكل ينظرون
وقيل لي ان اكتب ما اريد ولا أريد
وقام واحد منا يطالب بالبصل
كلها بصيلات ما يريد
وتجللت أسارير السعادة
واجب.
ثلاث بصيلات اتت مع الصباح
وثرت
أين الحقوق
والكل ينظرون ولا يجيبون
عوجة ما في عوجة ما في سعادتك
وجاء يوم سبت آخر
أول اسبوع وشهر آخر
وجاءوا ينثرون الرمل فوق العيون
فوق بيوت النمل ينثرون ويمسحون
ويكنسون.
وجاءوا على عجل
اليوم يوم المرور
وجاء يوزع البسمات في كل صوب واتجاه
عوجة ما في
عوجة ما في سعادتك عوجة ما في

وقام واحد منّا جديد
يطالب بالجديد
يطالب بالدستور بالحقوق بالقانون
وكلهم ينظرون
عليه أن يكتب ما يريد
وقيل لي اليوم دورك يا فلان
سعادتك البصل نريد البصل
سمعتني أقولها من قرب بعيد
وتجللت أسارير السعادة مرتين
فقد وعيت الدرس مرتين
وأصبح الصحن على أربع بصيلات
أربعاً كالقمر كتفاح الجنة كلهن
أخفيت إحداهن
زرعتها وسقيتها وعشتها حتى نمت
ذدت عنها الطير والأقدام
واخضرت الساحة وازدهت
حديقتي حديقتي حديقة الحيطان
قد نمت
والتف حولها الحديث والكلام والمكان والزمان
وصارت الرمز لنا
رمز النمو والحياة والأمل

مفتول العضل كالثور منه العنق
طويل الجسد
لسحنته مفعول الليل في نفوس الصغار
مقطب ما بين حاجبيه يمشي وينظر
التمام وينفخ في صفارته بينما يدور الآخرون حولنا يعدّون
يزفر في ضجر
دائما ترقدون دائما ترقدون
لا إعتبار عندكم لأحد
الشر من عينيه ينفذ الشر له عيون
أتى ذات صباح يحمل ورقة
هيّا الى المستشفى
وكان يمسك بالقائمة
رأسا على عقب
اي اسم آخر في القائمة
يسألني على جانب من الساحة
ن لا يعلم الآخرون بانه لا يقرأ

كان يلعن ويتوعد كل مسجون
ويل للمنتظرين من غضبته
حتى جاء يوما يطلب شيئا
من زيت كافور لدي
وعندها سقط القناع
وصار يلعن ويسب ويلعن
جهة أخرى ويزفر
يسأل عن حالنا
ويرسل السلام تلو السلام
عندما علموا بحاله
وأحالوه الى جهة أخرى
لعله مسجون هو الآخر
لعله مسجون

اصفّوا خمسات خمسات
كيف ونحن لا نزيد عن ثلاثة
أعرف أنكم ثلاثة
ولكن اصطفوا خمسات
خمسات خمسات
وجلسوا القرفصاء
وعدّكم واحد اثنين
ثلاثة
وقال هكذا تكون الخمسات
هكذا دائما تجلسون ونفخ
في صفارته لجماعة أخرى
وصار يعد ويعد ويعد
وينفخ في صفارته ويعد

حمدان يا سجن يا مسجون يا سجّان
يا سجن يا مسجون يا سجان
يا سجن يا مسجون يا حمدان
يا سجن يا مسجون يا سودان
حمدان يا مسجون يا سودان

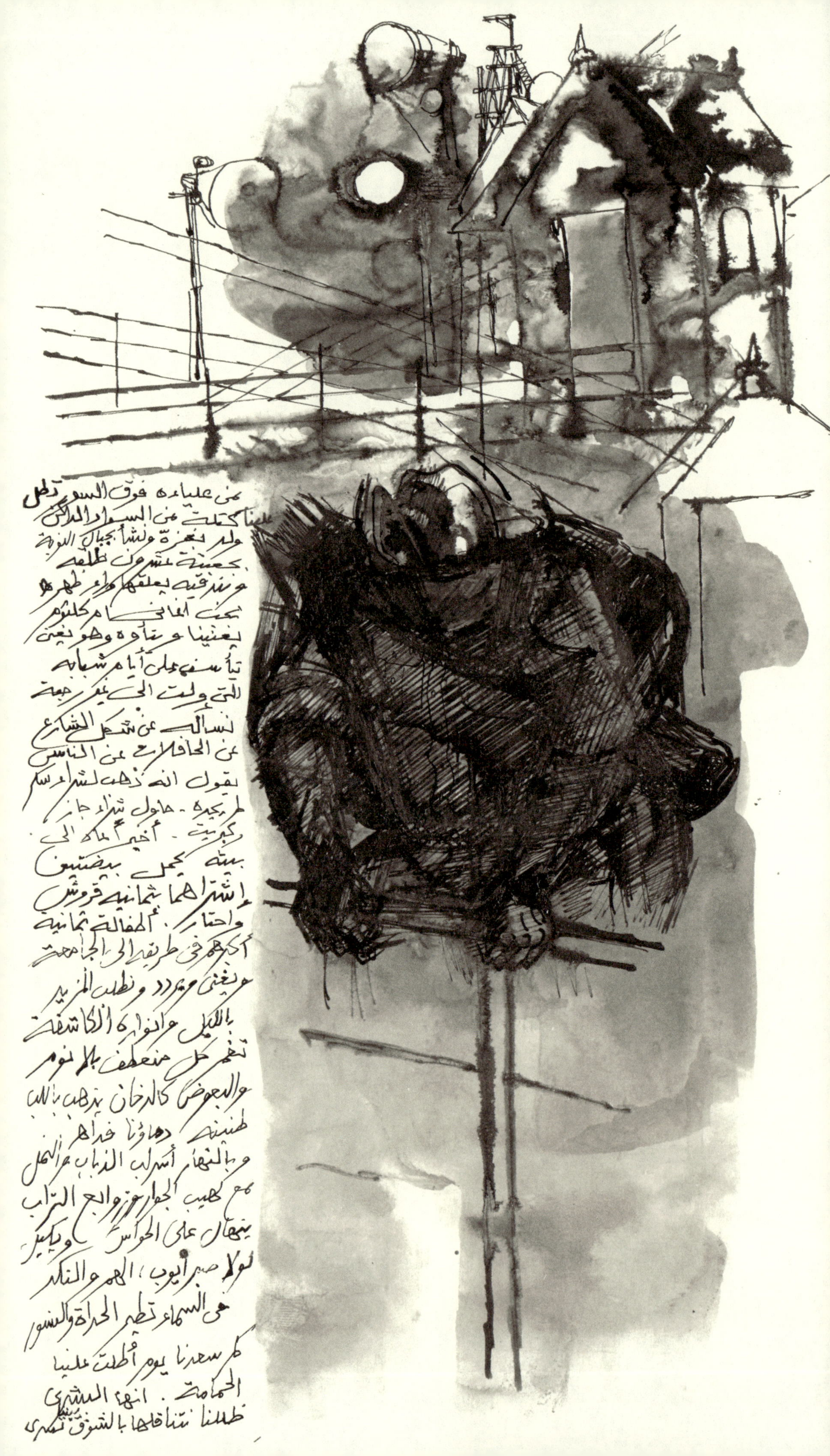
من علياءه فوق السور تطل
علينا كتلة من السواد الداكن
ولد بغزة ونشأ بجبال النوبة
بجبهته عشرون طلقه
وبندقية يعلقها وراء ظهره
يحب أغاني أم كلثوم
يغنيها ويتأوه وهو يغني
يتأسف على أيام شبابه
التي ولت الى غير رجعة
نسأله عن شغل الشارع
عن الحافلات عن الناس
يقول انه ذهب لشراء سكر
لمركبه . حاول شراء جاز
وكبريت . أخيراً أخذ ماله الى
بيته يحمل بيضتين
إشتراهما بثمانية قروش
واحتار . أم الطفالة ثمانية
أكبرهم في طريقه الى الجامعة
ونغني ويردد ونطلب المزيد
بالليل وانوار الكاشفة
تغمر كل منعطف بلا نوم
والبعوض كالدخان يذهب بالبال
طمأنينة دهاؤنا خداع
وبالنهار أسراب الذباب والنمل
مع لهيب الحر وزوابع التراب
ينهال على الحواس ويكبر
لولا صبر أيوب ، الهم والنكد
من السماء تطير الحداة والنسور
كم سعدنا يوم أطلت علينا
الحمامة . انها البشرى
ظللنا نتناقلها بالشوق لمصري

وكان يوم الاثنين الثامن من سبتمبر عام خمس وسبعين وتسعمائة بعد الألف الميلادي
الذي يوافق الثالث من شهر رمضان عام خمس وتسعين وثلاثمائة بعد الألف الهجري
وعند منتصف النهار من يوم قائظ الحر
أتى اثنان من رجال الأمن العام
لأحدهما أوداج منتفخة كالقيمات
صدقات موسمي الأثرياء

وذهبت معهما لا ألوي على شيء
ورميت داخل زنزانة مفردة سبقني
إليها من استفرغ ما في جوفه كله وأفاض
وأغلق عليّ بالمزلاج والضبة والطبلة والمفتاح
وأتى من وراء القضبان
من يأخذ تفاصيل اسمي للمرة الرابعة
وأخبرت أن أوراقي تحت الطبع
سأحال اليوم إلى المعتقل بسجن كوبر

لا إله إلا أنت سبحانك إني كنت من الظالمين
وإنا لله وإنا إليه راجعون ولا حول ولا قوة إلا بالله العلي العظيم
وسرت خلال أبواب الحديد والحراس
والبنادق إلى ساحة السجن
بيتي الجديد. وإلى حين
التراب أول ليلة توسدته ساعة النوم
بجواري يرقد أستاذ للفلسفة بجامعة الخرطوم
وأستاذ في الذرة وغيره من كبار رجال القضاء
والمحاماة وقادة الحركات النقابية العمالية
واتحادات الطلاب كبارهم وصغارهم
ورجالات الأحزاب والطوائف وغيرهم وغيرهم وغيرهم

سمعته يحكي قصته وهو يضحك
والجميع يشاركونه الضحك حتى اغرورقت
أعينهم بالدمع. أحد قادة العمال كان ويكون
لقد فزت على مرشح الجماعة في الانتخابات
العامة ولم أسمع لتوجيهات السلطة
وأنا لهذا معكم.
وبدأ الغطاء ينزاح عن بصري شيئاً فشيئاً وبالتدريج بدأت أبصر

عن كوننا نقبع المحكوم عليهم بالإعدام
في انتظار التصديق شنقاً
بالنهار في منتصف لا صوت كلام
ولا حفيف
يسهرون الليل في الحديث
والغناء والدوبيت والحديد

ومن ليسا بإزار اثنان
حيث يعدونهم للموت
وحجرة التنفيذ
حبل معلق من سقف وفراغ أجوف التجويف
"أنا أخوك يا فاطمة"
"أنا أخو البنات"
"أنا أخو البنات"
"أنا أخو البنات"

وعند الفجر نسمع الصوت، نسمع الحديد

في الرابعة بالتحديد
يا إلهي كم نسمعك
جلياً كمولد طفل، جلياً كالقدر
كم نسمعك جلياً نسمعك من وراء الجدران
ويقال أن الرقبة تطول
تطول كالجمل، تطول تجاه وادي الحرية الأبدي

ويقف العسكر صفاً صفاً صفوفاً متراصة صفاً بعد صف

سبعة أبواب من الحديد

نعبرها بعد تفتيش دقيق

للخروج للتحقيق هيّا أسرعوا هيّا يا مساجين النكد

وتعاد الكرّة عند الخروج

عند الفجر

وفي الرابعة بالتحديد

سعيد الحظ منّا من يعود

سعيد الحظ منّا من يعود

سعيد الحظ منّا من يعود

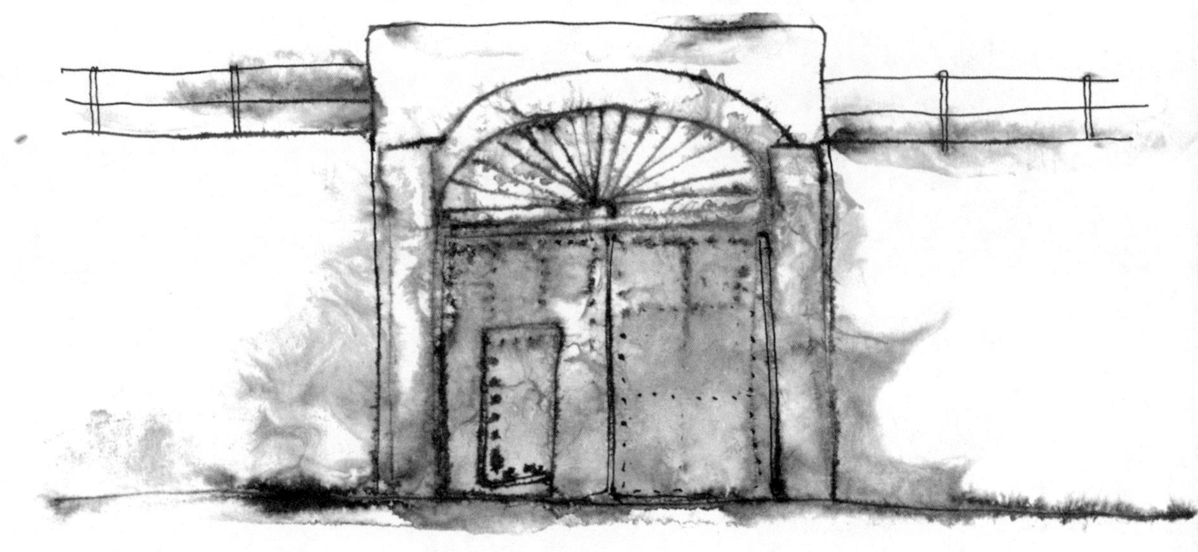

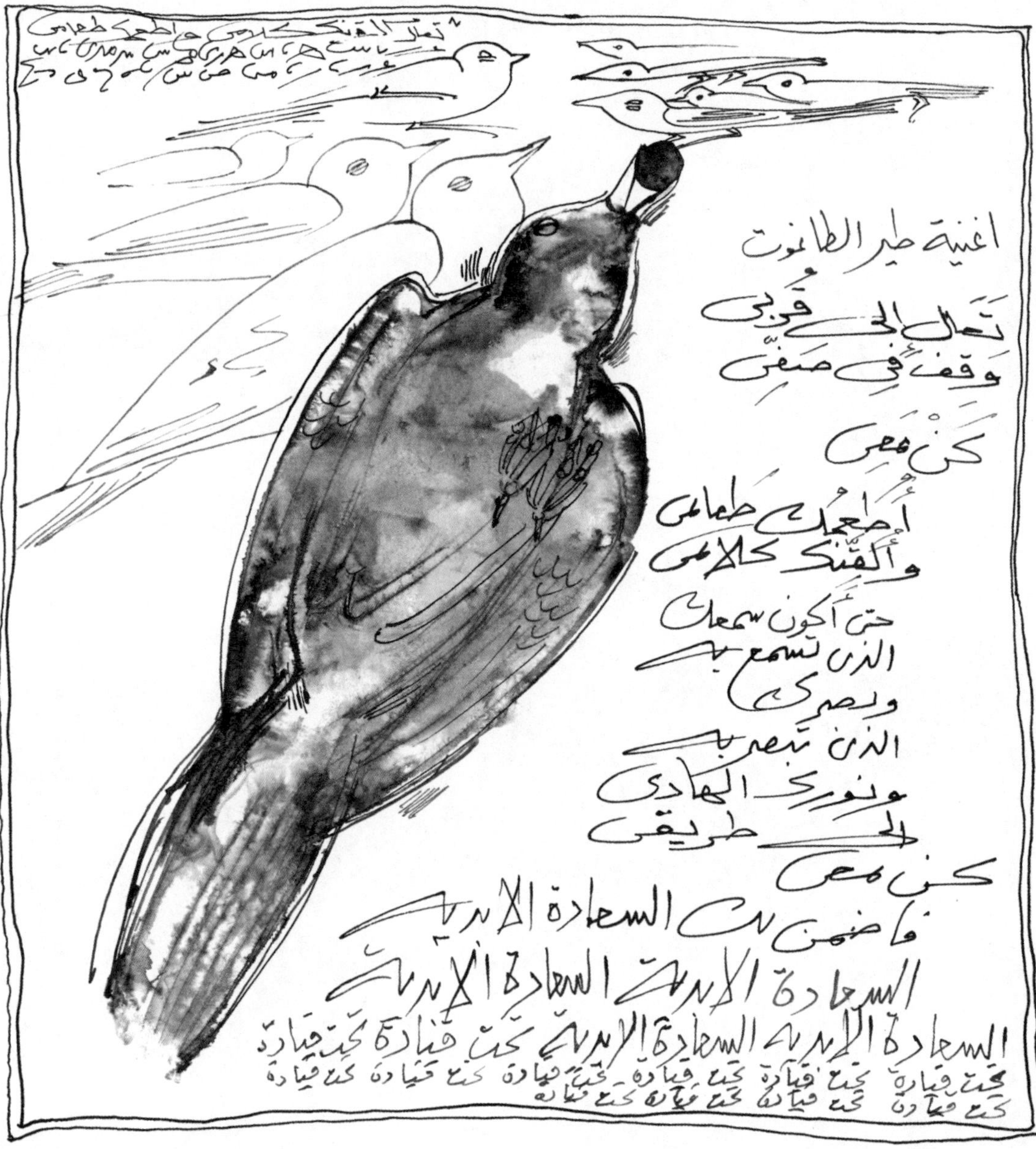

اغنية طير الطاموت

تعال الى قربي
وقف في صفي

كن معي

أطعمك طعامي
وألقنك كلامي

حتى أكون سمعك
الذي تسمع به
وبصرك
الذي تبصر به
ونوري الهادي
الى طريقي

كن معي
فاضمن لك السعادة الابدية
السعادة الابدية السعادة الابدية
السعادة الابدية السعادة الابدية تحت قيادة تحت قيادة
تحت قيادة تحت قيادة تحت قيادة تحت قيادة تحت قيادة تحت قيادة

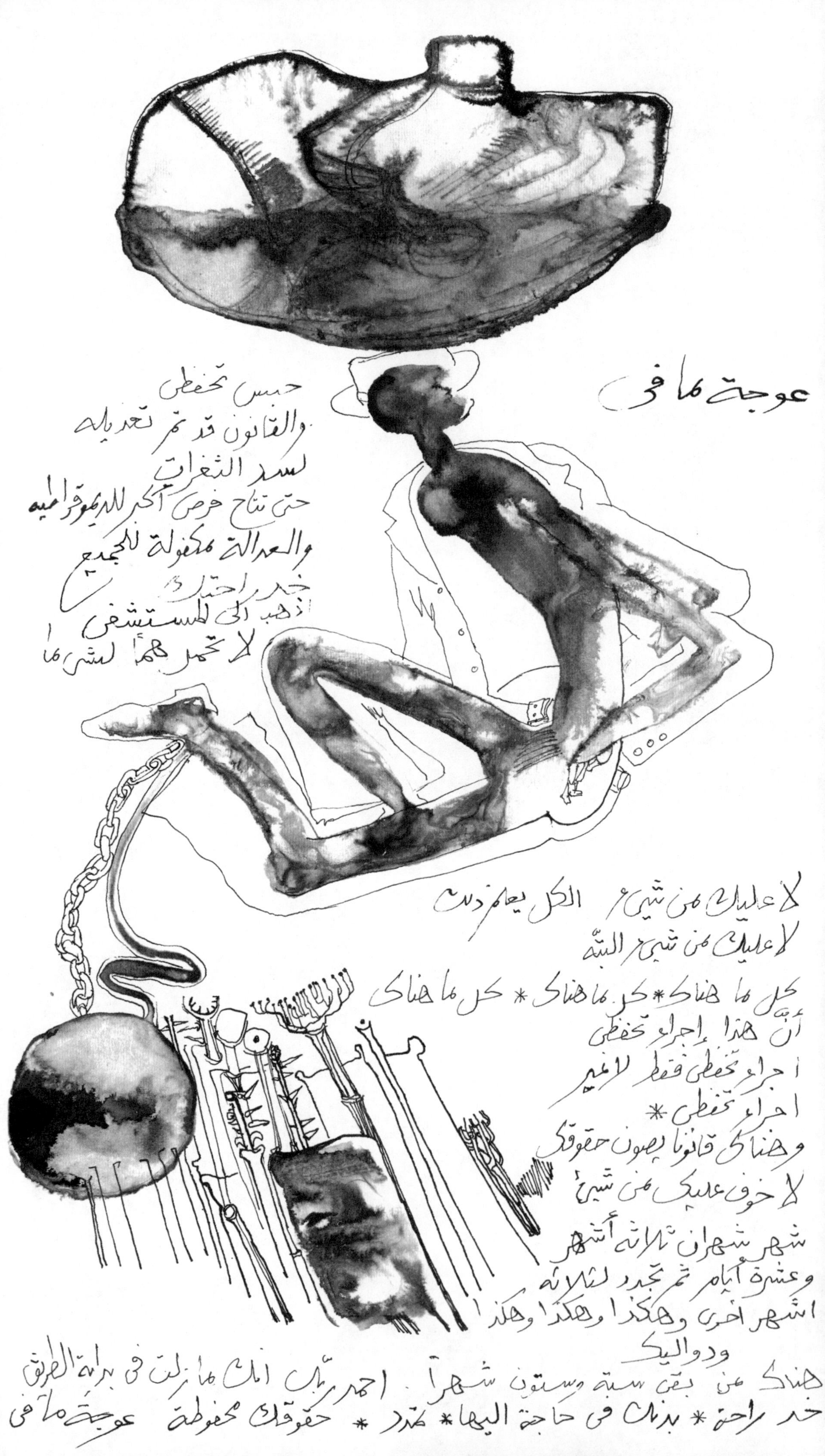
عوجة ما في
حبس تحفظي
والقانون قد تم تعديله
لسد الثغرات
حتى تتاح فرص أكبر للديموقراطيه
والعدالة مكفولة للجميع
خذ راحتك
اذهب الى المستشفى
لا تحمل هماً لشيء ما
لا عليك من شيء الكل يعلم ذلك
لا عليك من شيء الله
كل ما هناك * كل ما هناك * كل ما هناك
أن هذا إجراء تحفظي
إجراء تحفظي فقط للأمن
إجراء تحفظي *
وهناك قانوناً يصون حقوقك
لا خوف عليك من شيء
شهر شهران ثلاثة أشهر
وعشرة أيام ثم تجدد لثلاثة
اشهر أخرى وهكذا وهكذا وهكذا
ودواليك
هناك من بقي سنة وستون شهراً . احمد ربك انك ما زلت في بداية الطريق
خذ راحة * بدنك في حاجة اليها * هدد * حقوقك محفوظة عوجة ما في

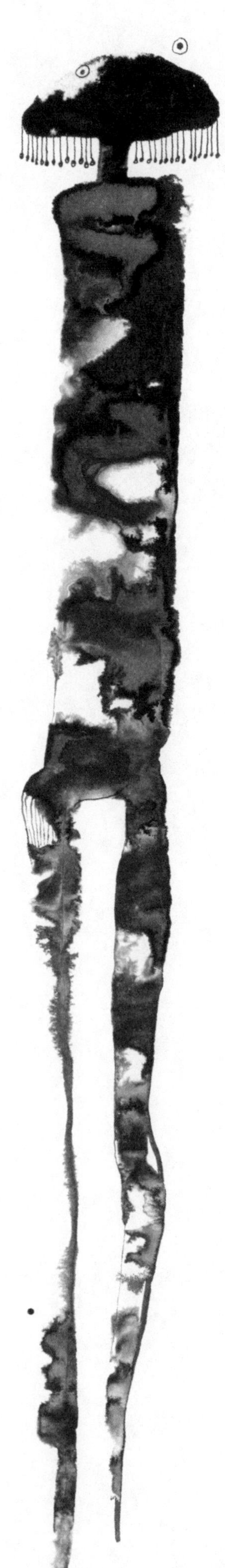

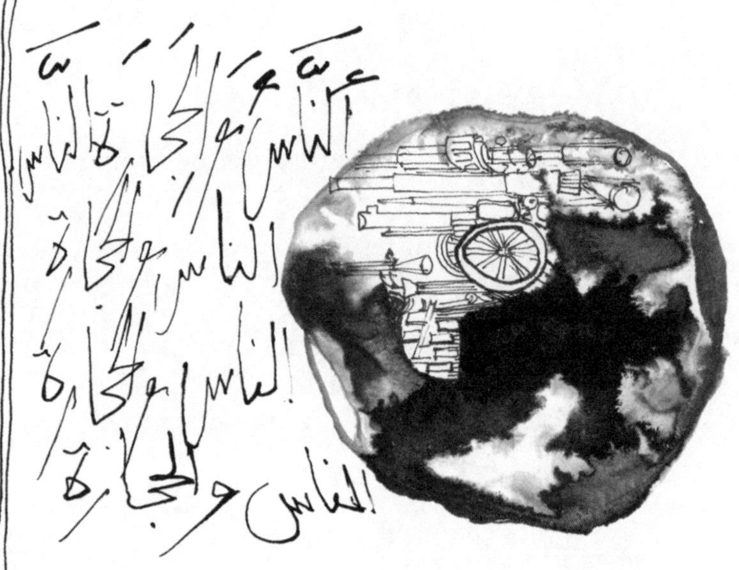
الناس والحجارة الناس
الناس والحجارة
الناس والحجارة
الناس والحجارة

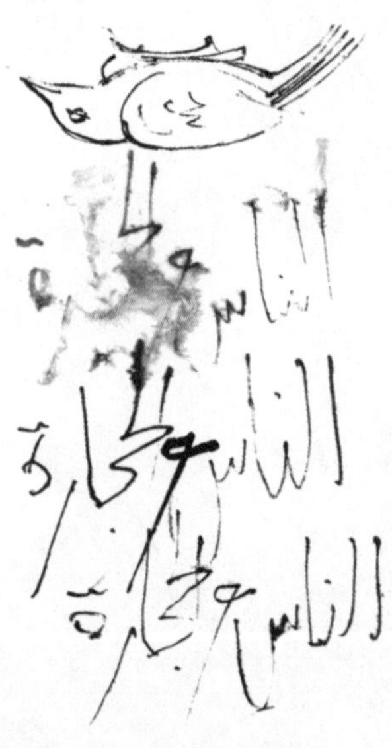
الناس و
الناس والحجارة
الناس والحجارة

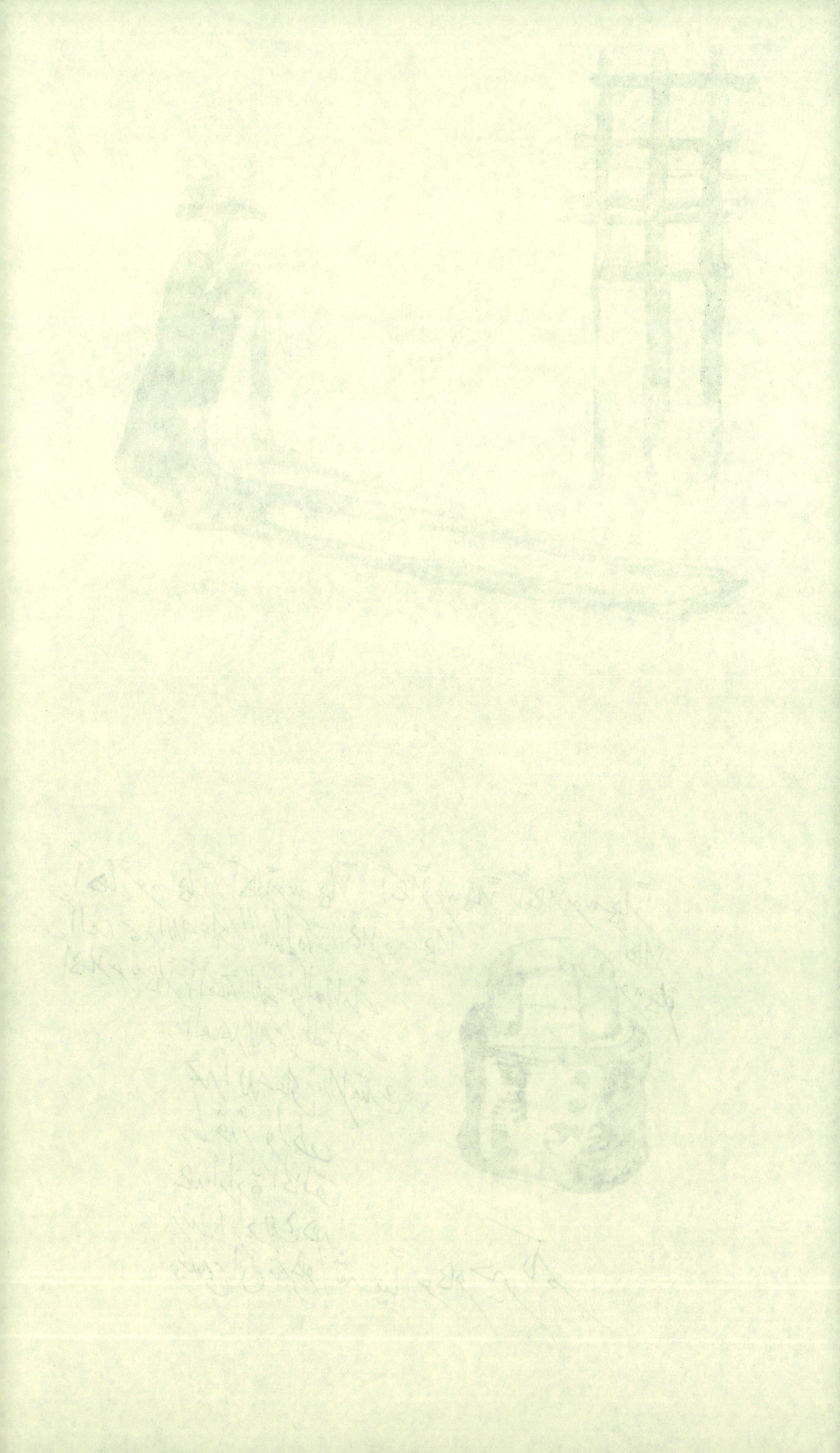

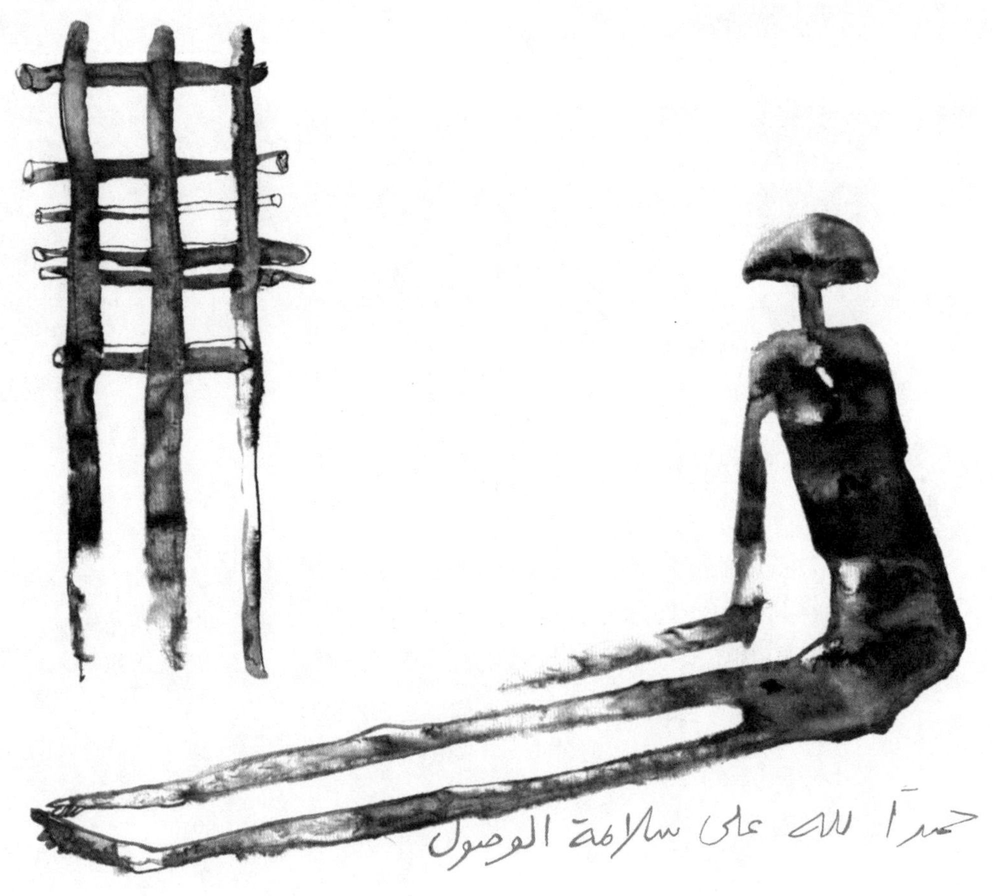

أهلاً وسهلاً أهلاً وسهلاً أهلاً وسهلاً أهلاً وسهلاً أهلاً وسهلاً

ألف حمد الله على السلامة أهلاً وسهلاً

أهلاً وسهلاً ألف حمد الله على السلامة

ألف حمد الله على السلامة

حمداً لله على سلامتك

ربنا قدّر ولطف

هذه إرادة الخالق

ربنا أراد لك هذا

وعسى أن تكرهوا شيئاً وهو خير لكم

أهلاً وسهلاً

ادخلوها بسلام آمنين ولا تيأس من رحمة الله

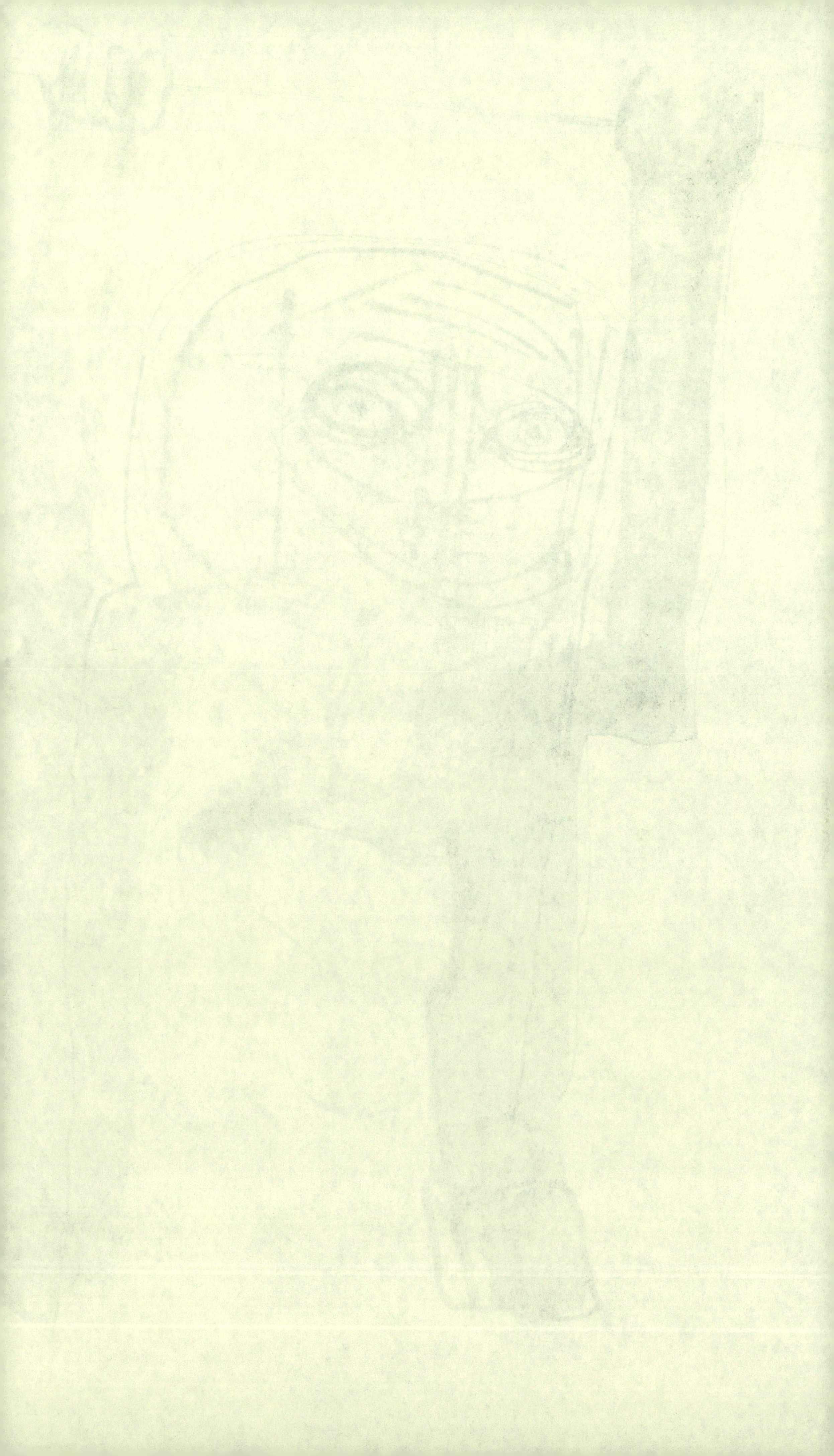

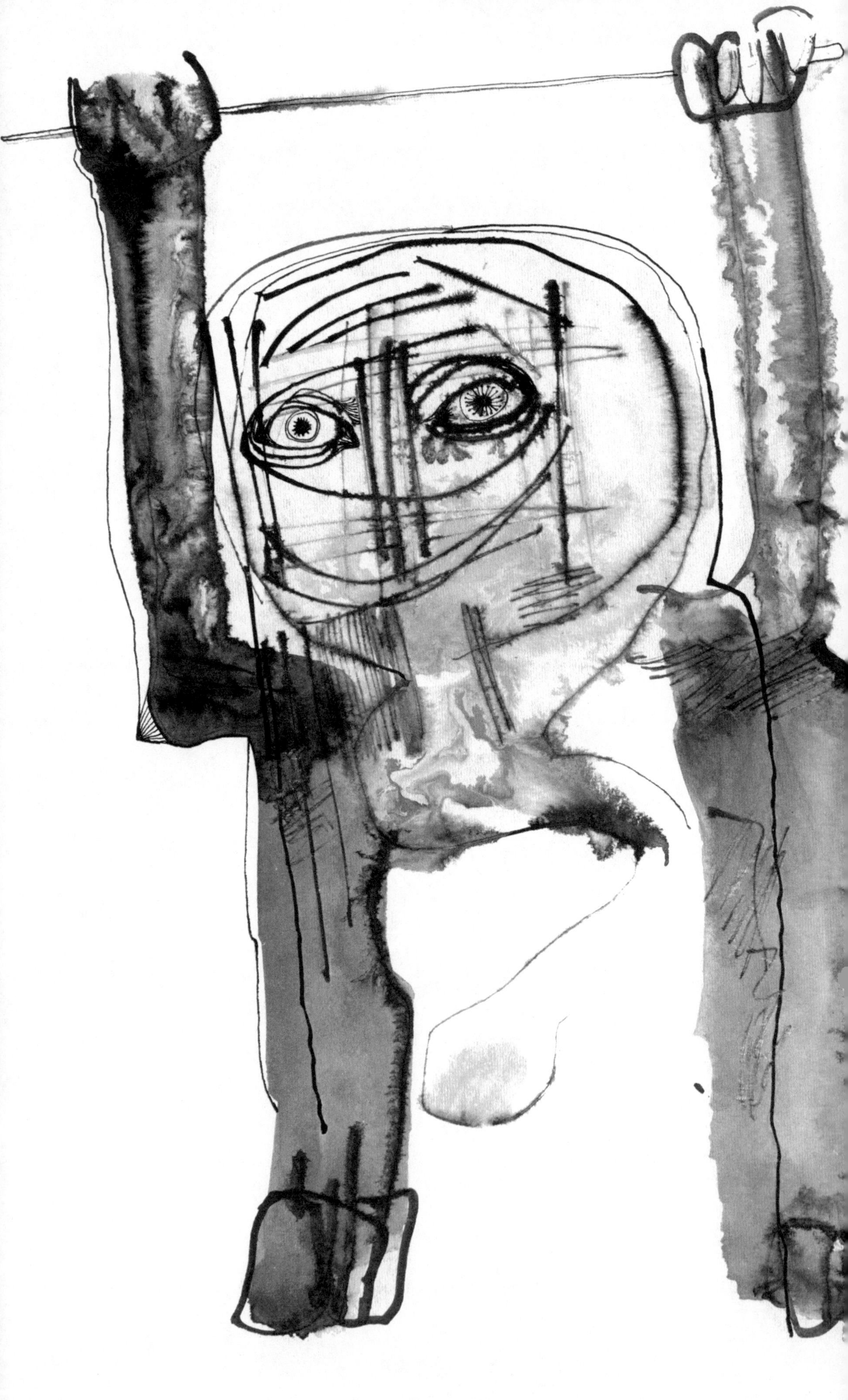

كلها دقيقتان وتعود إلى أهلك

ومضت ستة أشهر
وأنا وراء القضبان ما
وجدران ظلما تطاول السماء

ولا أرى أحداً
إلا من كان حظهم
مثلي والحراس
كلنا سواء

مزلاج أبواب الحديد
يصك الأذن صداه
كالرعد هديره الرعد له هدير
بلا ذنب جنيناه بلا ذنب جنيناه بلا ذنب

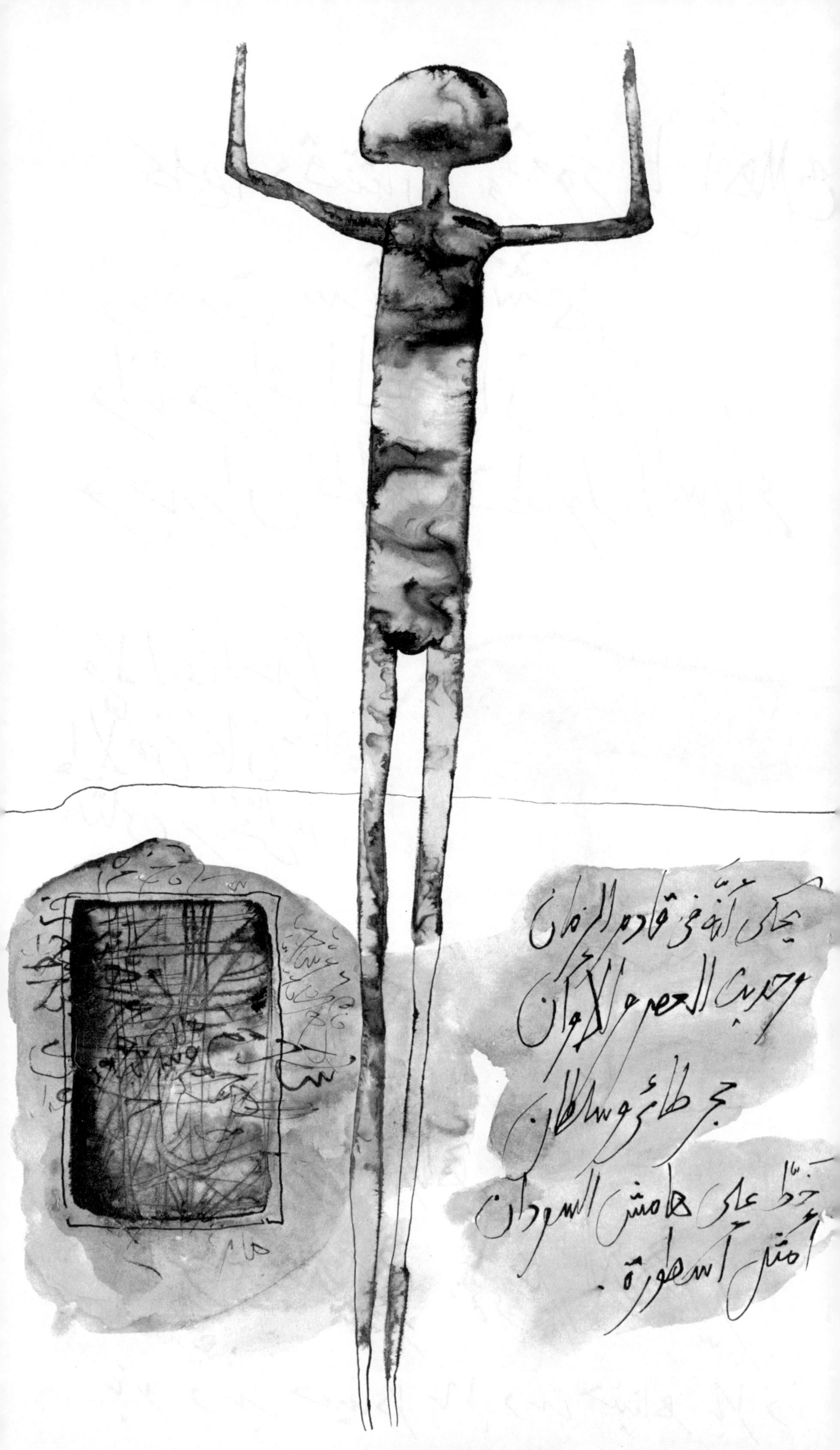
يحكى أنه في قادم الزمان
وحديث العصر والأوان
حجر طائر وسلطان
خط على هامش السودان
أمثل أسطورة .

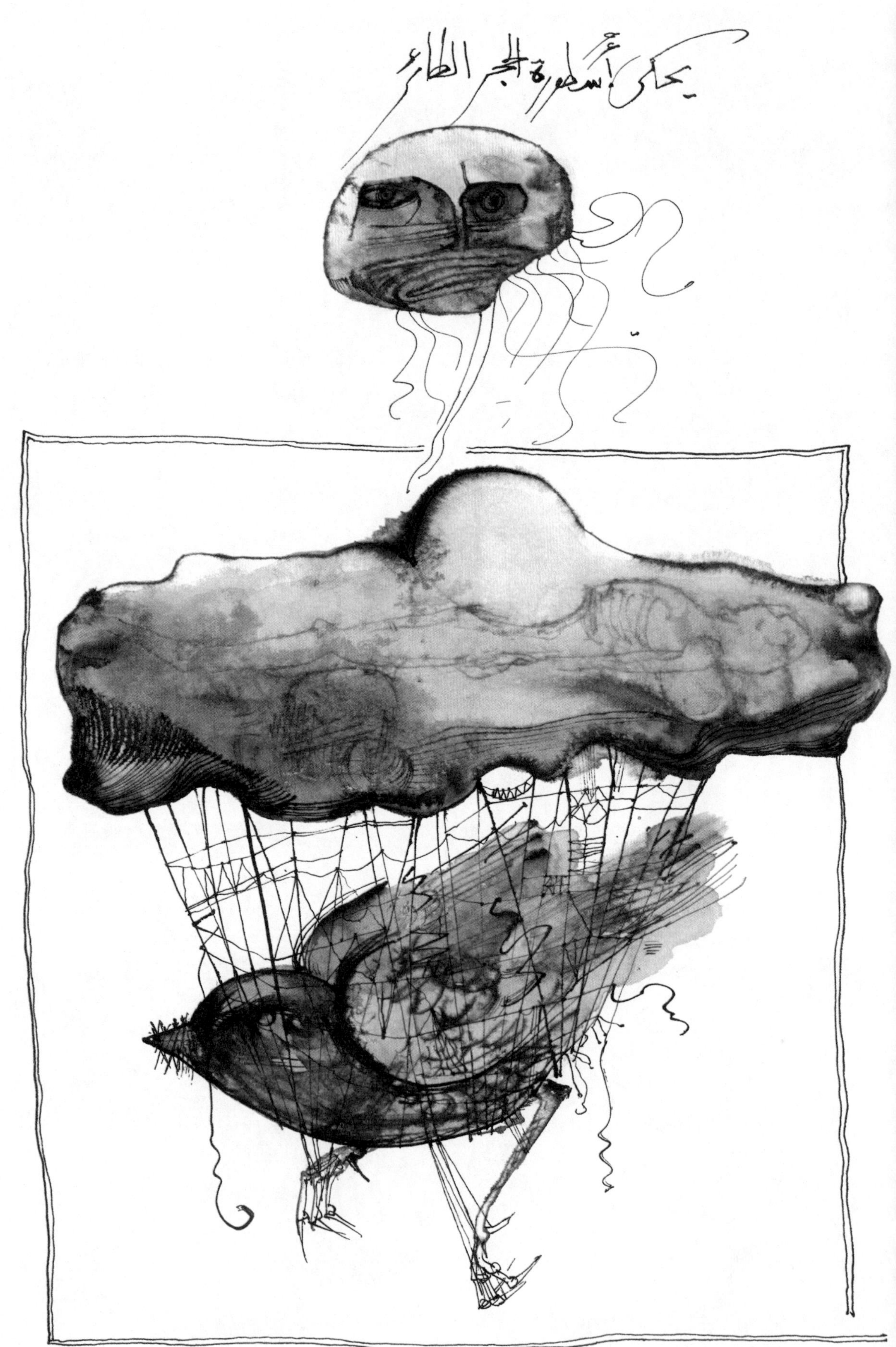
يحكي عن أسطورة الحجر الطائر

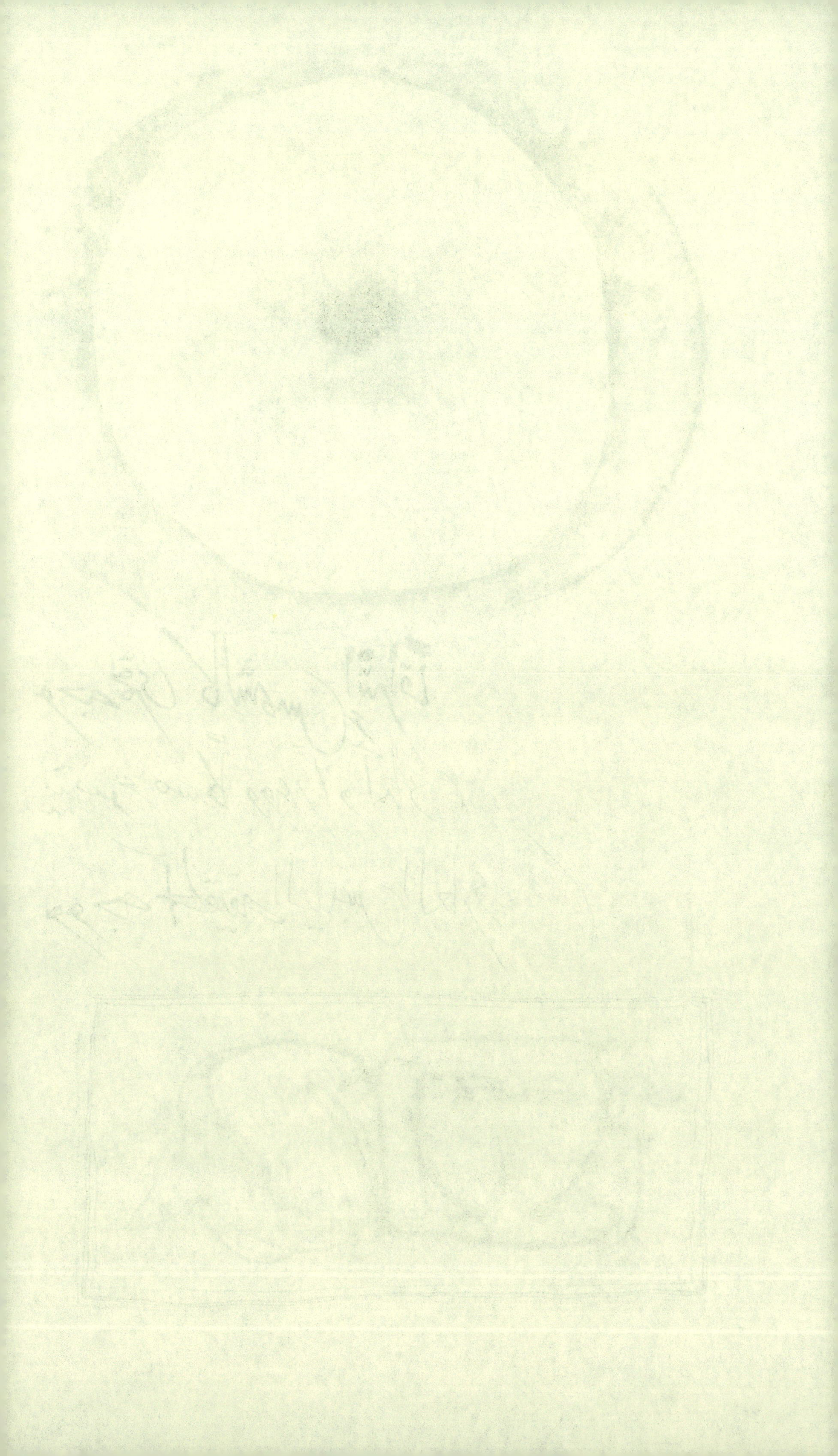

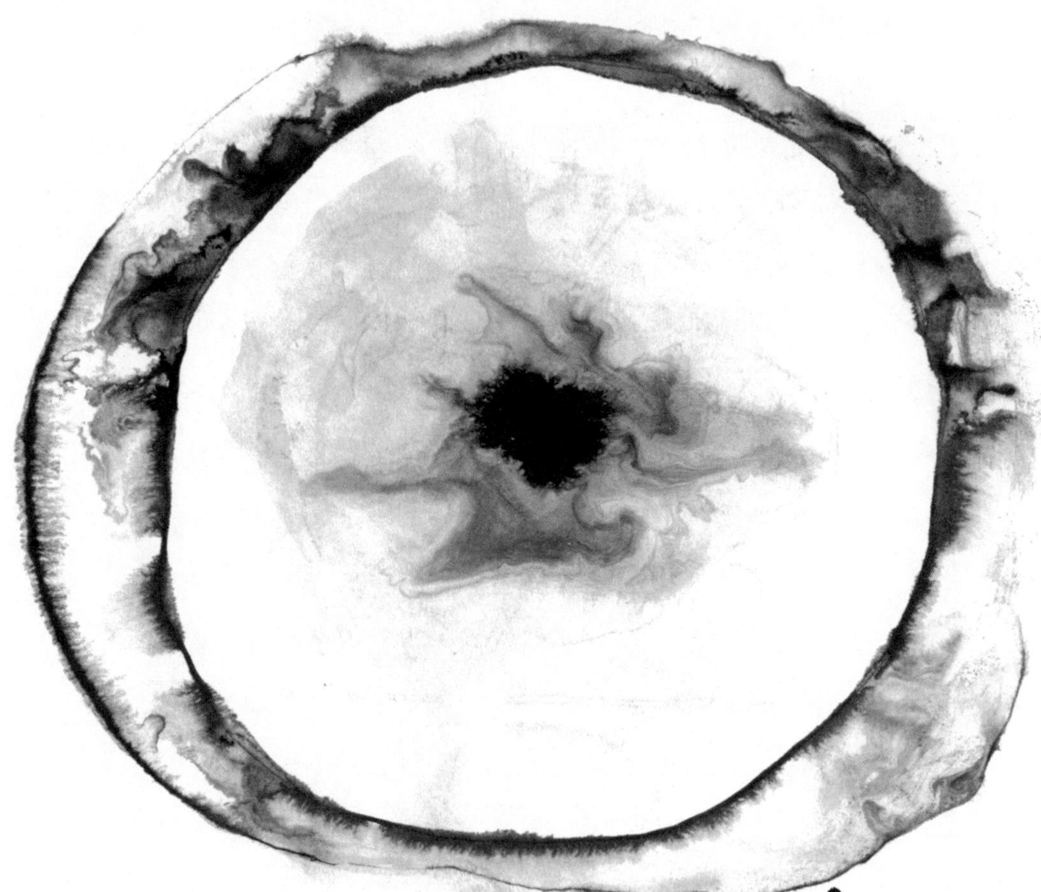

وجه قمري كالشمس إشراقاً
يتضوع مسكاً ووعداً وأماني
ووجه الحقيقة اليابس العاري

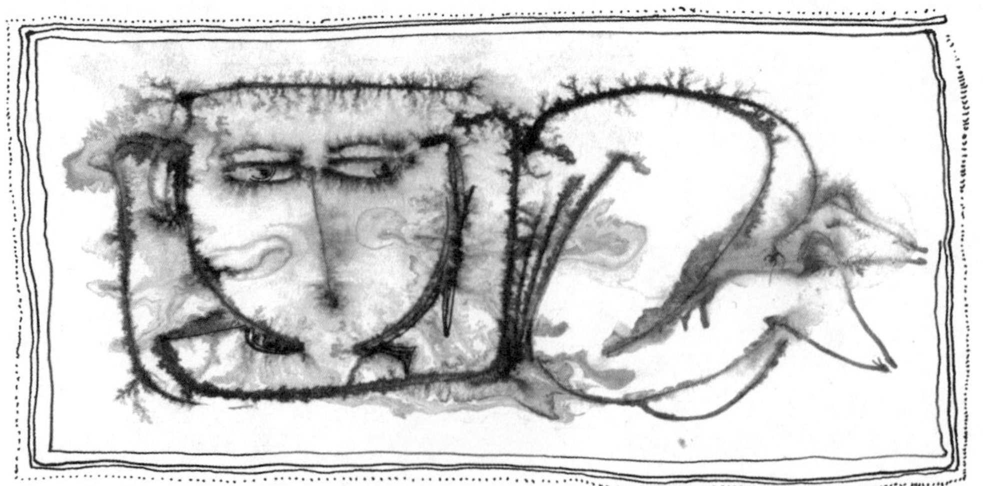

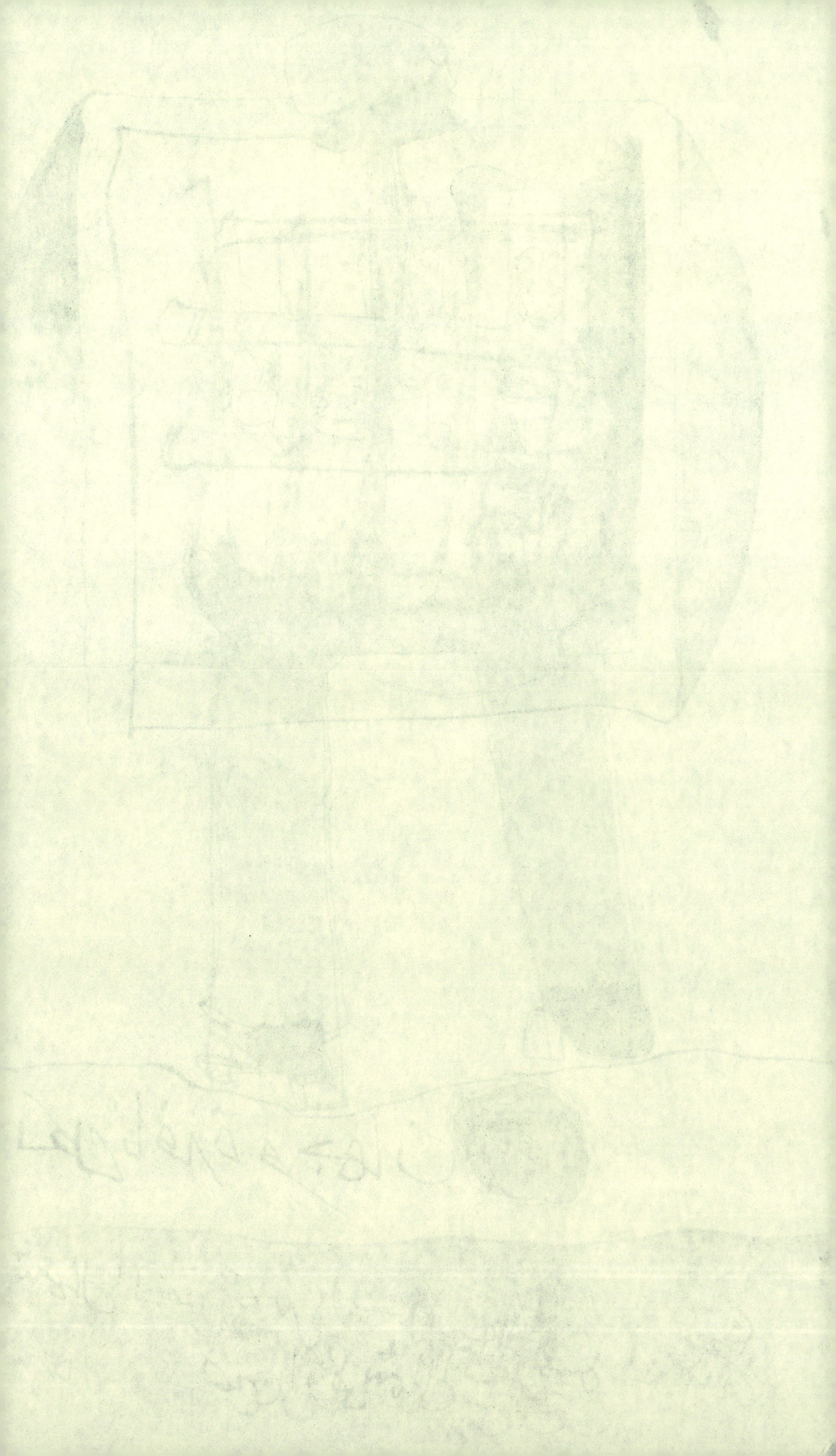

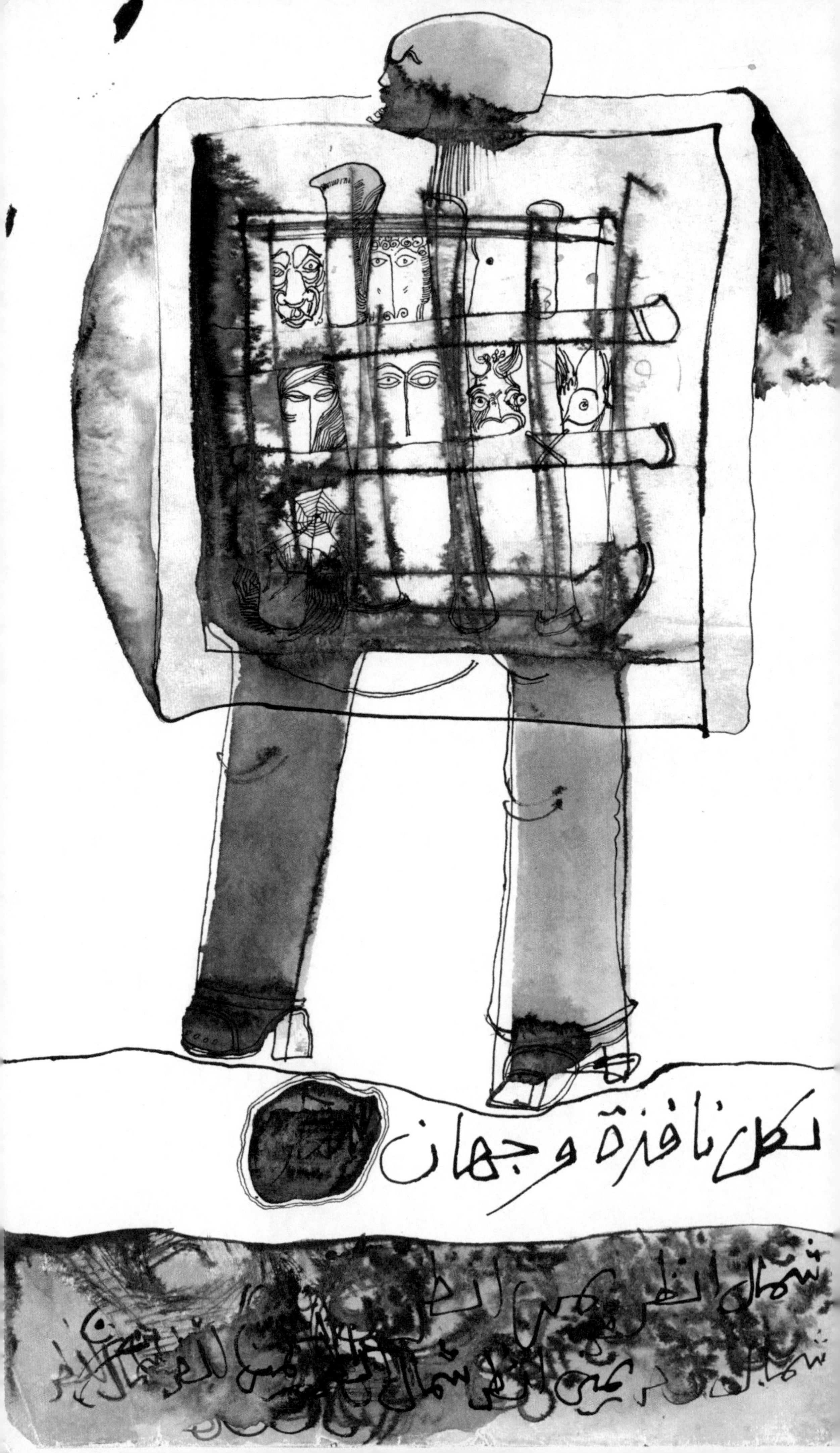
لكل نافذة وجهان